Dance with th

Li

This book is dedicated to the two greatest women in the world: Bette & Katie.
Thank you for your never-ending faith, encouragement, and love.
Duane & Don

Published by Dance with the Elephant L. L. C.
26440 Hermitage Road
Cold Spring, MN. 56320
(320) 980-4625
DancewiththeElephant.org

Photo Credits:
Front Page & Inside Cover Elephant Art - Alexandra Evens, After Credit Page Black & White Elephant Art - Ashley Tong
55 - Sam Kuss, 81 - Mona Steinke, 89 - Bette Kuss, 107 - Donald Cahoun, 121 - Donald Calhoun, 145 - Duane Kuss, 147 - Duane Kuss,
166 - Ashley Tong, 167 - Ashley Tong, 167 - Black & White Elephant Art - Ashley Tong

All other photo images Dreamstime LLC (www.dreamstime.com) Pages: Credit Page - Ambientideas, Before Contents Page - Dmitry Pichugin,
2 - Zacarias Pereira Da Mata, 8 - Sergey Galushko, 9 - Amith Nag, 10 - Amith Nag, 12 - Kelliem, 14 - Tebnad, 16 - Vicki France,
18 - Ian Wilson, 20 - Louisafonso, 22 - Ghadel, 24 - Taigis, 26 - Isabel Poulin, 28 - Neil Bradfield, 30 - Pavalache Stelian,
32 - Tose, 34 - Diego Vito Cervo, 36 - Cammeraydave, 38 - Geno Sajko, 45 - Denis Polikarpov, 46 - Corey A. Ford, 48 - Jakub Cejpek,
50 - Rolffimages, 52 - Paul Topp, 54 - Skypixel, 56 - Cammeraydave, 58 - Sinastraub, 59 - Franciscah, 60 - Maxim Petrichuk,
62 - Fotoksa, 64 - Mian61, 66 - Steven Prorak, 70 - Daveallenphoto, 72 - David Coleman, 74 - Yuryy Bezrukov, 76 - Daveallenphoto,
78 - Paul Moore, 80 - Maxim Samasluk, 82 - Tomgriger, 83 - Anton Sokolov, 84 - Christopher Meder, 86 - Sebastian Schubanz, 88 - Jason Vosper,
90 - Tupungato, 94 - Roberto1977, 96 - Richardseeley, 98 - Laurentiu Iordache, 100 - George Muresan, 102 - Johannes Gerhardus Swanepoel,
104 - Orlando Florin Rosu, 106 - Cumpah, 108 - Ryan Stevenson, 110 - Ron Chapple, 112- Paura, 114 - Ekaterina Pokrovsky, 116 - Jennbang,
118 - Alekuwka, 120 - Monkey Business Images, 122 - Udra11, 127 - Nathaniel Luckhurst, 128 - Agsandrew, 130 - Purmar, 132 - Gordon Logue,
134 - Bowie15, 136 - Michal Bendarek, 138 - Vladi Samodarov, 140 - Linda Morland, 142 - Jose Gil, 144 - Cammeraydave, 146 - Jerry Sanchez,
148 - Jcsphoto, 153 - Lunamarina, 154 - Norma Chambers, 156 - Lorenlewis, 158 - Anna Berkut, 160 - Cesar Robles, 162 - Serge Villa,
166 - Juan Jose Tugores Gaspar, 167 - Tomo Jesenicnik, 168 - Alain Lacroix, 169 - Pavel Losevsky, 169 - Ambientideas

Elephant Adapted Artistic Illustration Pages 31, 37, 45, 53, 57, 65, 72, 115, 141, 152, 161 - Alexandra Evens / Donald Calhoun
Life's Cosmic Equation Illustration Pages 33, 47, 71, 95, 129, 155 - Donald Calhoun

Legal: Michael R. Vadnie, Esq.

Design: Don Calhoun
Editor: Lauren L. Murphy

Printed and bound in The United States of America: Sentinel Printing Company, St. Cloud, MN. 56304

DANCE WITH THE ELEPHANT
"BECAUSE YOUR LIFE IS WORTH IT!"

"Dance with the Elephant *is a journey of self-discovery, connecting with others and finding your Cosmic Legacy."*

Duane Kuss & Don Calhoun

Contents

Introduction: Don's Story in Stone

*"We look forward to the time when the Power of Love
will replace the Love of Power.
Then will our world know the blessings of peace."*

William Ewart Gladstone

It was my first day back to work since my brother Bob had unexpectedly passed away. My primary mentor in life, the man I considered as my second father, the guy I always aspired to be like, was taken away from me in an instant; he just fell down one day in his cabin and died at age sixty-three. For the first time in my life, I, the professional memorial counselor, was faced with the sobering reality my clients bring to me every day: the fact that death and the loss of loved ones suck! The reality was that I was still suffering a bushel basket of grief, and my mental state was in no way ready to handle the emotional anguish of another grieving client.

But sometimes miracles happen, and the moment you feel like the storms of life are about to drown you in sorrow, someone throws you a life jacket of hope. That morning, a couple walked through the office door that had traveled a hundred miles to see me. I had never met Kris and Rod before, but our coming together that day was surely divine providence. The same week my brother had died, they too suffered a startling loss. Their son Miles, a strapping young man on the high school wrestling team, had suddenly collapsed and died during a wrestling match. He had been born with a rare heart defect that remained undetected until that fatal moment on the mat, in front of all of his teammates. The parents, still in shock and consumed by their grief, were looking to find a memorial that would appropriately represent their cherished son.

We were three weeping souls that auspiciously came together that day and poured our buckets of pain and suffering onto the floor of my office. Normally it's my job to ask penetrating emotional questions to help clients dig deeper into the meaningful stories of their loved ones. I instinctively act out of love and caring for the grieving family. But that day was different. That day, I desperately needed love and support for the loss of my brother as much as Kris and Rod looked for comfort with their son. We were mutual guiding spirits and established a trusting bond together that would buoy us over the next couple of months as the memorial design process for their son's monument evolved.

During our final meeting together Kris turned to me out in the parking lot and looked directly into my eyes: "Don, thank you for helping me understand and process Miles' death. You, better than anyone inside or outside my family, helped me connect to the loving gift he still is to me." I replied that fortuitously she had done the same and helped me rise from the emotional abyss of my brother's death to understand how his spirit stills lives in me. Together, we remembered the gifts, lessons, and stories that both Bob and Miles gave to life. We gave honor and respect to the legacy of their lives and recognized their unending spirits within us.

Death, grieving widows, funerals, and cemeteries were all a part of growing up for me. I was born the youngest son of a monument builder. My father, a monument company owner and salesman, made his living by meeting, advising, designing, and manufacturing cemetery monuments (more commonly referred to as tombstones). Every week, he would hit the road calling on grieving widows and widowers throughout Minnesota. As I grew older, my dad would even take me along on sales calls, using me as an ice breaker and a deal closer with clients.

I remember as a self-righteous young teenager thinking that my father's profession was not very respectable. I had a hard time accepting the reality that he was making a living off of the tragedy and death of others. Ironically, after college, I decided to follow in my father's footsteps, and I soon came to understand my father's passion for his noble profession. I came to understand death as a gift and blessing. Every human being, from the very moment of birth, has a destiny card punched with a time to die. Death is just a reality of life and it is a gift that helps us anchor the understanding, appreciation, and value of living in the moment. For the past thirty years, I have built my career around helping people connect with the stories that represent their loved ones and finding ways to represent those legacy memories on a granite memorial.

I take my memorial counseling role —helping people find ways to cope with their loss and emotional despair—very seriously. Most of the people I deal with are struggling to find purpose and meaning in the tragedy and death of their loved one. To connect at a deep emotional level, I have to find ways to build trust and respect with people very quickly. Fortunately, I have always had a gift for effortlessly bonding with my clients. In a matter of minutes, I have families openly sharing their life stories involving love, joy, and happiness. Sometimes they share their deepest, darkest secrets that include fear, hate, anger, guilt, and shame.

Later in this book, the topic of death denial in Western society will be addressed at great length, but for now it's important to understand the influence it had on writing this book. As a memorial counselor, I meet people from all walks of life trying to navigate the cascading river of death and grief. People may intellectually say they understand that death is a part of life, but, unfortunately, their emotional behavior does not mirror this reality. Death in our society is treated like a secret. Fear of death, is the "elephant in the room" that no one ever wants to talk about. Throughout my career, I have come to realize that the cultural norms of Western society strongly position death as something that happens only to the other guy: "If I ignore it, maybe it will go away."

Of even greater concern is the fact that most caregivers, those who deal with death on a daily basis, don't have the training, support, or energy to handle the emotional trauma of helping people deal with death. From medical staff to morticians, the challenge of dealing with death and the difficult choice of connecting with people at a deep emotional level require a great amount of effort and energy. It's much easier to focus on the process and the procedures of the job than it is to demonstrate true empathy and compassion for clients. Can you blame them? How would you like to deal with the emotional baggage of death and dying every day? Living in a society where death is always the elephant in the room, how would you stay motivated to face another family consumed by loss and grief?

Here are just a few of the stories I witness every day:

*A family tells me that their ninety-three-year-old mother's death was such a shock. How old is old enough to die respectfully?

* I was on a national board of all the major leaders in the death industry. I almost laughed out loud when a prominent and respected leader said, "If I die, I want a unique and creative funeral." I hate to tell you that there is no "if" in death.

* A son was filled with so much hate and disrespect for his deceased father that he adamantly refused to pick up the cremated remains at the funeral home.

* A man who visits his wife's grave every day for five years straight still consumed by the guilt of not having been at her side when she fell out of bed at the nursing home.

* A man, in a fleeting moment witnesses the horrific death of his wife as a semi-truck, splits their car in two on the highway. Who is prepared to support him emotionally?

Time after time people sit in front of me telling stories of loved ones who were disconnected from personal purpose and meaning in life. The purpose of this book, however, is not to battle in the trenches of tragedy and death but instead to discover new ways of living a more fulfilling life. The paradox you are faced with is the fact that the cultural beliefs about avoiding and running from death are obstructing your ability to truly appreciate life. By learning to understand and accept the meaning of death, you can discover the true gift and purpose of choosing how to live.

As we begin this self discovery journey together it is important to note that Dance with the Elephant: Life's Cosmic Equation is a part of a Life Equation trilogy. Humankind participates in life at three different levels of interaction. These are known as the "Me," "We," and "What Will Be" phases of life. Each phase is defined by a combination of universal inputs that are added and multiplied to create a simple formula for choosing your life's journey.

These include:

"ME" – Life's Quantum Equation
(Imagination + Intuition + Hope) * Action = Life's Destiny

"WE" – Life's Cosmic Equation
(Creative Power + Receptive Choice + Faith) * Time = Life's Legacy

"WHAT WILL BE" – Life's Revelation Equation
(Dreams + Knowledge + Love) * Exploration = Life's Discovery

In this book we'll probe deeply into the "We" phase of life's journey. It will begin with the realization that nothing in the universe stands alone. Everything exists in unity with something else. Anything we do as individuals will always affect someone or something else. We will discover that there is a cosmic energy connection between all people and all things in the world. This underlying link will be explained using the Life Equation terms of Creative Power, Receptive Choice, Faith, and Time. We will come to understand how these four components drive our relationships and create the stories of life that become our Cosmic Legacy.

The Journey Begins

"Whatever you do, you need courage. Whatever course you decide upon, there is always someone to tell you that you are wrong. There are always difficulties arising that tempt you to believe your critics are right. To map out a course of action and follow it to an end requires some of the same courage that a soldier needs. Peace has its victories, but it takes brave men and women to win them."

Ralph Waldo Emerson

Book Design & Navigation

This book was designed to entice, engage, and challenge you immediately. If your reading style is to thoroughly examine page after page, cover to cover, you will discover a consistent flow between reflection-photo-quote pages, principal topics, and personal stories. If you'd rather jump through the book at random, you'll find the reflection-photo-quote pages on the left-hand side to be insightful and inspirational. This book was created to be a lifetime companion and not just a one-time wonder. As you grow, the interaction you'll have with this book will grow too.

The left-hand side of this book is designed for personal reflection and meditation. Let the impassioned photos and the inspirational quotes dance in your mind. Connect the reflection-photo-quote to a personal story in your life. Where might this combination take you in the future? Write it down! Commit to it! Take action toward it!

The right-hand side of this book is designed to be a personal discovery resource for your life's journey. The insightful topics and revealing stories will provide you a new framework for looking at life yesterday, today, and tomorrow. You have the opportunity to empower your future and to reach your designed destiny in life. Thank you for choosing to join us on this journey to your cosmic legacy.

Dance with the Elephant

"You've gotta dance like there's nobody watching,
love like you'll never be hurt,
sing like there's nobody listening,
and live like it's heaven on earth,
and speak from the heart to be heard."

William W. Purkey

We chose the title *Dance with the Elephant* as the foundation of our work for myriad reasons. No, it's not about you joining the circus and riding into the arena on top of the largest living land animal in the world to do the cha-cha. This is a self-help, self-discovery book designed to connect you with universal principles and forces in nature that shape your perception of reality. You will come to understand that your self-manifested purpose in life is a part of a relational dance among the polarities of human existence. Your journey through this book will guide you to ways of spirited dance with both the drama and the trauma events of life. You will discover the true value both the yin and the yang have in fulfilling your life's destiny and your universal cosmic legacy.

To dance is to move rhythmically to music. Music is a part of life, our world, and the entire cosmos. The ancient Greek and Indian philosophers defined music as tones ordered horizontally as melodies and vertically as harmonies. A more modern viewpoint describes the border between music and noise being a matter of cultural preference. There is no such thing as noise, only sound. "Music to my ears" is defined purely in the mind of the beholder. In this book, you'll come to understand that in order to dance you have to hear the music. The music is always playing; you just have to learn how to hear it. For every dance there is usually a series of steps and patterns to follow. The dance can involve a partner or even groups of people, all in rhythm with the music and with one other. At times, you follow your partner, and at times, you lead them. You will come to understand that in order to dance with the elephant you must dig deeper to find the "me" of life, and when you learn to grow deeper you can dance in harmony with the "we" of life.

The music that plays within me and the rhythm that vibrates between us is a direct connection to the emotional and mental states that resonate between us. When the music has a low frequency, resonating fear, distrust, shame, blame, and guilt, our physical bodies, along with our emotions, draw back and power down. The dance

*"You must live in the present, launch yourself on every wave,
find your eternity in each moment.
Fools stand on their island of opportunities and look toward another land.
There is no other land; there is no other life but this."*

Henry David Thoreau

can become spasmodic and might stop completely. When the music resides in the higher frequencies of love, joy, passion, and inspiration, the energy flows freely between us, and our awareness expands to include all the beauty that the universe has to offer. The dance is in harmony, and the unified creative power evokes new life discoveries. But the true test lies in the fact that the music of life has both low and high frequencies, both conscious and subconscious, and the challenge is to learn how to dance to all the vibrations of the cosmos.

Earlier, we introduced the elephant in the room as the fear-of-death syndrome in Western society. The "elephant" is usually the unspoken emotional secret in the room that everyone is aware of but nobody is willing to talk about. Unfortunately, these secrets that are never openly discussed continue to fester and rankle in the unconscious mind. Eventually they become roadblocks in our lives that limit the options we consider and the choices we make. Essentially, these secrets prevent us from reaching for and achieving our cosmic destiny. It is the premise of this book and the entire Dance with the Elephant Series that, by learning to talk about the elephant-in-the-room secrets, we free ourselves from the shackles of the unknown and the trepidation that comes with it. Just by verbalizing the secret, its power and control diminishes.

The spectrum of life is filled with dramatic moments and traumatic moments. Too often we bury these events deep in our unconscious seemingly to protect ourselves. When you learn to Dance with the Elephant, you dig deeper into conversations to discover the drama and you grow deeper with people to uncover the trauma. Ultimately, learning how to dig deeper and grow deeper will bring greater meaning and purpose to your relationships in life.

The elephant is also a wonderful metaphor for many other facets of human existence. There are many similarities to elephants and humans. Elephants can live up to seventy years in the wild. Baby elephants are the center of attention in the

"All Finite things have their roots in the infinite, and if you wish to understand life at all, you cannot tear out it's context. And that context, astounding even to bodily eyes is the heaven of stars and the incredible procession of the great galaxies."

W. MacNeile Dixon

elephant herd and rely on their mothers for as many as three years. They communicate by touch, sight, and sound. Elephant intelligence has been compared with that of primates, and they appear to have self-awareness, even to the point of showing sympathy for dying or dead individuals of their kind. The elephant's color is not black or white but rather shades of grey, allowing it to represent the middle ground between the binary extremes of the universe (good vs. bad, pain vs. pleasure, love vs. grief, life vs. death).

Elephants have been revered by human culture as far back as Paleolithic times. Rock paintings and engravings of the animal are found in Africa from this era. They have been the subject of numerous religious beliefs throughout Africa and Asia for thousands of years. Even modern-day Western politics identify the elephant as the symbol of the US Republican Party. Elephants are commonly used in children's stories and represent models of high character and exemplary behavior. And certainly we all can remember the role of the magical circus elephant and many pictures it painted in the minds of young and old for the past century.

To dance with the elephant is to connect with the origins of the universe. You were given the seed of life at birth and your purpose is to plant it in fertile soil, water it, and nurture it that someday it might bear great fruit. Your destiny is to break loose from the cultural norms that have tied you down in the past and to discover your personal creative power. You'll learn how to beat the rhythm of your own drum and to dance to your own music. After strengthening the "me" in your life, you'll reach out to the "we "of humanity by gathering a strong core of friends who can join you in a new dance together. Your core group will be entering into an agreement, a "Circle of Trust" (COT) covenant, with the purpose of helping each other grow. Your COT group will support you with the insight and wisdom to pursue your dreams and to reach your destiny. Together you will dance with the elephant and thereby fulfill your Cosmic Legacy in the universe.

The Four Pillars

*"If one advances confidently in the direction of his [or her] dreams,
and endeavors to live the life which he [or she] has imagined,
he [or she] will meet with success unexpected in common hours."*

Henry David Thoreau

WARNING . . . DANGER . . . CAUTION . . .
Do you have the curiosity, passion, and tenacity needed to learn how to Dance with the Elephant?

The Dance-with-the-Elephant experience is not for everyone. We believe that only one in ten will be brave enough to take this journey. To test your fortitude for the challenge, there are four pillars of understanding that support the walls of this special world. You must agree to each of the four pillar principles in order to comprehend and apply the visionary tenets presented throughout this book.

Think of it like Dorothy's adventure in the *Wizard of Oz* story. Your journey will include Dorothy, the Scarecrow, the Tin Man, and the Lion. All four will provide you guidance for how to follow the yellow brick road on your journey to the world of "Dancing Elephants." The place where your dreams can come true and your personal Cosmic Legacy will be discovered.

Respect

The world you live in is saturated with cultural binaries and dualities: black and white; right and wrong; big and small; best and worst; allies and enemies. Just take a moment and think about all the contrasts that pummel you every day. In order to exist and function as human beings, each of us begins to digest the world at a very young age and unconsciously establishes accepted norms and social principles that, in effect, define our personal binary extremes. Since birth, most of us have lived with parents, siblings, and relatives who had certain traditions, values, and norms. The group of people you live with are located in a geographical location that has a dominant culture, religion, and societal framework. All of these pieces of the puzzle play a role in forming your personality, character, and temperament. To exist within a social system, one must conform to the norms and values of that system.

"The glory of friendship is not the outstretched hand, not the kindly smile, nor the joy of companionship; it is the spiritual inspiration that comes to one when you discover that someone else believes in you and is willing to trust you with a friendship."

Ralph Waldo Emerson

- What are the characteristics of an emotionally strong woman versus a weak one?
- What determines a man who is a good provider compared to a worthless bum?
- How much money does it take to live on the rich side of town?
- How poor do you have to be to live on the other side of the tracks?

The daily judgments you make based on social bias spin a subconscious web of security around you. Societies exist to provide a framework under which people can live from day to day without going stir-crazy.

To Dance with the Elephant you must first come to RESPECT the need for every person to create their unique mental balance and way of looking at life in a world of endless dualities. All of us have done our best to create a stability in life as best we can, based on the genetics passed down to us from our parents and the environment in which we grow up. Each human being deserves to be treated with high regard, admiration, and honor, just because they exist. There is no such thing as the need to earn respect or to satisfy a series of cultural prerequisites. Just the very presence of another living, breathing person merits your respect for their inherent dignity.

Respect means that you have the desire and ability to recognize value, worth, and virtue in others. Although their story and life experiences will very likely be different from yours, you will resist the need to judge them, knowing there are always new ways of thinking about and observing the world around you. Paradoxically, until you can truly respect and appreciate the people you have the opportunity to connect with in life, you'll find it impossible to honestly love and accept yourself. You can't give what you don't already have. Respect is a gift that, when you learn how to dance with the elephant, you give freely.

Should you choose to learn how to dance with the elephant, as you travel down the yellow brick road, your journey will likely include many roadblocks, detours,

"If you once forfeit the confidence of your fellow citizens, you can never regain their respect and esteem. It is true that you may fool all of the people some of the time; you can even fool some of the people all of the time; but you can't fool all of the people all of the time."

Abraham Lincoln

and "under construction" signs. You will be faced with all of life's favorite emotional road bumps, including guilt, shame, blame, and self-criticism. All the demons of your past will have the chance to surface their ugly heads during your personal pilgrimage through this book. But instead of allowing these emotions to run rampant in your mind as they most likely have in the past, here you'll have a road map to follow. You'll discover a way to respect your life experiences and accept them for what they are. The process will empower you to make choices today that will leverage your natural Creative Power and move you toward a more fulfilling life destiny.

Your individual life experiences and perceptions have great value. It is important for you to respect your personal journey and story for the magnificent contribution it has and will make to the world. Like a single grain of sand you see while walking along a beach, each tiny pebble plays an equal part in contributing to the beach as a whole. Respecting someone else's journey demands a personal desire for you to be open to the perceptions of others, even if they are diametrically opposed to your own. Respect requires the use and practice of active listening skills. It demands that you invest your time and energy into the relationship because you know there's significance there and value in their story. They too are a rare and important grain of sand found on the seashore.

Guiding Principles to Dance with the Elephant: RESPECT

- ☑ Everyone is entitled to their own opinions and feelings.
- ☑ Dance participants are encouraged to use active listening skills.
- ☑ Try to always gain clear and accurate understanding of each dancer's point of view.
- ☑ Try to be as optimistic and positive as possible with those you dance with.
- ☑ Be willing to invest your time and energy to improving the life of your dance partner and the dance team.

*"Respect means that you have the desire and ability
to recognize value, worth, and virtue in others."*

Don Calhoun & Duane Kuss

Trust

The second pillar holding up walls of the "great elephant ballroom" is called TRUST. Trust provides the confidence, faith, and conviction that your journey down the yellow brick road of life will have purpose and meaning. You must trust in yourself, and you must trust in the people you meet along the way.

Having trust in the people who are closest to you, believing that they will always try to look out for you, having your best interest in mind is all-empowering. Giving trust to people you meet in life and sincerely looking into their eyes as they share their story with you will build bonding relationships that can last forever. Similar to respect, trust must be assumed and given freely at the outset. It should never be used as a reward or enticement. Trust is the glue that bonds your connections with people. To give and receive trust unlocks the door to a life of growth and personal fulfillment.

A part of the Dance-with-the-Elephant journey is to trust in yourself and the people closest to you so that together you can begin to deal with the elephant in the room. Slowly but surely you can discover and expose the secrets in life that have silently controlled you and have limited your personal growth and freedoms. You can begin to melt down the shame, blame, and guilt in your relationships through honest and clear disclosure of what you perceive and how you feel. Trust will provide you the confidence to look in the mirror and see yourself for who you truly are: the good, the bad, and everything in between. You can then help others see themselves in the mirror and provide support as they uncover their skeletons in the closet and their hidden secrets.

So will you be the one in ten who will risk to trust in yourself? Will the strength of your personal trust be strong enough to reach out to other people in your life with

"Yesterday is gone.
Tomorrow has not yet come.
We have only today.
Let us begin."
Mother Teresa

Dance with the Elephant: Life's Cosmic Equation

unconditional trust and acceptance? The challenge is great, but the rewards are infinite.

Guiding Principles to Dance with the Elephant: TRUST

☑ Each dancer is expected to enter the dance fully trusting each other.
☑ Each dancer is expected to be completely honest and as clear as possible in expressing themselves.
☑ Each dancer is expected to vocalize any concerns or misunderstandings he or she feels needed to be clarified at any point during the dance.
☑ Mean-spirited and derogatory comments aimed at destroying, shaming, or guilting another dancer will not be tolerated.

The Desire for Growth

Take just a moment to close your eyes, take a big deep breath, and think about the four seasons of the year: spring, summer, fall, and winter. What pictures pop into your mind when you visualize each season? Add your thoughts to the list below:

Spring: buds, blossoms, rain, birds, bees
Summer: warm sun, big leaves, full bloom, flies, mosquitoes
Fall: harvest, fruit, leaves falling, bird migration, boxelder bugs
Winter: cold, snow, ice, quiet, dormant, mice

Now let's explore the life cycle of an apple tree during the four seasons. In the spring, the buds on the apple tree that were dormant all winter, explode with new growth, developing blossoms, leaves, and new branches. The blossoms entice bees and other insects to help in pollinating the tree, the leaves will grow to provide photosynthesis nutrients for the tree, and new branches will help the apple tree expand and capture more sunlight to grow bigger and juicier apples during the

*"I prefer to be true to myself,
even at the hazard of incurring the ridicule of others,
rather than to be false,
and to incur my own abhorrence."*
Frederick Douglass

summer and fall. As we move into summer, blossoms become fruit, leaves grow to full-size and maximum nutrient production, and the new branches thicken and strengthen to support the weight of the apple fruit. During the fall, the apples mature for harvest, new buds develop on the branches for the coming year's growth, and the leaves dry up and fall to the ground, providing nutrients for the tree's root growth in future years.

You, like the apple tree, are destined to experience all the seasons of life. You, like the apple tree, will have different kinds of growth depending on the season. You will have a time to grow branches and a time to bear fruit. You, like the apple tree, are intended to reach for the stars at night and to delight in the comforting warmth of a bright sunny day. To learn to dance with the elephant is to understand the purpose of continuous personal growth throughout the seasons of life. And like the bees and other insects that help pollinate the apple tree, you need people in your life to help you grow and develop through the seasons. People who respect, trust, and nurture your personal growth in life are the natural outcome of learning how to dance with the elephant. Welcome the help of others. This is not something you can do on your own. Establishing, growing, and confirming your relationships with family and friends are an important part of this journey.

Do you feel it? Can you hear it? The dance is already beginning to emerge. Do you aspire to learn and become more with each day of life? Is there a place deep within you that provides the courage and strength to explore new ideas and concepts? Welcome to the dance team! You have made an empowering choice. Your simple determination to place one foot down in front of the other will guide you to dancing with the cosmic energy vibrations of the elephant. By applying the principles of dancing with the elephant to your life, your dreams can become your reality and legacy. Because your life is worth it!

"I am not bound to win, but I am bound to be true.
I am not bound to succeed, but I am bound to
live up to what light I have."

Abraham Lincoln

Guiding Principles to Dance with the Elephant: DESIRE FOR GROWTH

☑ Each dancer is expected to carry the desire for personal discovery, growth, and exploration while learning to dance.

☑ Each dancer is expected to help others in their desire for discovery, growth, and exploration.

☑ Growth, by its very nature, requires risk. Each dancer should be dedicated to creating as healthy, open, and risk-free an environment as possible.

☑ The key is to develop a clear understanding of all the dancer's perceptions, actions, and beliefs. This is the reason people do what they do. Resist judging others based on your values and beliefs. Your life is your life. Their life is their life. Through better communication, however, you will be able to go from the perspective of "me" to "we" and ultimately to "what will be."

Confidentiality

In the world of lawyers, doctors, and therapists, a commitment to confidentiality requires that information shared by a client with the professional representative is not to be shared with others. This is important in building an environment of trust between the patient and the counselor. In the journey of learning to dance with the elephant, a similar commitment to confidentiality is made between you and those with whom you choose to share your experiences.

As you proceed along the journey of digging deeper into the "elephants" of your life and grow deeper in dancing and learning with others, it is important to remember that it is all a part of the learning process. Exploring your past—your dreams, disappointments, emotions, and feelings—takes courage and risk.

A part of dancing with the elephant involves taking a look into the rearview mirror of your past. You will revisit the highs and lows: dreams, accomplishments,

"Allow yourself to think only those thoughts that match your principles and can bear the bright light of day. Day by day, your choices, your thoughts, your actions fashion the person you become. Your integrity determines your destiny."

Heraclitus

failures, disappointments. It will be important to know up front that, whomever you invite to be a part of your circle of trust, they will be required to respect total confidentiality within your group. The goal of dancing with the elephant is to experience the positive release and freedom you'll feel when the secrets, hurt, blame, shame, isolation, and guilt of the past can be talked about openly. You and you alone will choose the pace by which the secrets bound by the chains of the past will be discovered and explored.

The four pillars of respect, trust, desire for growth, and confidentiality provide a solid foundation to begin your journey. If you have the strength and courage to adhere to these tenets as you explore the contents of this book, you will be rewarded by learning how to dance with the elephant and move to all rhythms that life has to offer you.

Guiding Principles to Dance with the Elephant: CONFIDENTIALITY

- ☑ The stories, emotions, feelings, and dreams expressed are considered to be confidential in nature among your "Circle of Trust" group, unless expressed otherwise.
- ☑ Any breach of confidentiality without the express permission of any of the other members of your COT group is not permitted.

Learn more about the Four Pillars at <u>DancewiththeElephant.org</u>

Life's Cosmic Equation

*"Despite the enormous quantity of books, how few people read!
And if one reads profitably, one would realize how much stupid
stuff the vulgar herd is content to swallow every day."*

Voltaire

LIFE'S COSMIC EQUATION

Life's Cosmic Equation is one in a series of three insightful equations we developed to help explain the purposeful role each of us plays in the universe. The origin and inspiration of the equations were discovered inside the combined works of Pulitzer Prize-winning anthropologist Ernest Becker, historian Thomas Berry and his colleague cosmologist Brian Swimme, and the epic philosophical work of prolific author Ken Wilber.

All humanity is involved in life at three different levels of interaction. These can be described as the "**Me**," "**We**," and "**What Will Be**" phases of life. Whether or not you're aware of it, you are simultaneously contributing to each of these levels during the journey of your life and even after your death. Each of these levels has its own components that combine to create a unique and purposeful life equation.

"ME" – Life's Quantum Equation
(Imagination + Intuition + Hope) * Action = Life's Destiny

"WE" – Life's Cosmic Equation
(Creative Power + Receptive Choice + Faith) * Time = Life's Legacy

*"Twenty years from now you will be more disappointed by
the things you didn't do than by the ones you did.
So throw off the bowlines. Sail away from the safe harbor.
Catch the trade winds in your sails.
Explore. Dream. Discover."*

Mark Twain

"WHAT WILL BE" – Life's Revelation Equation
(Dreams + Knowledge + Love) * Exploration = Life's Discovery

This book will introduce you to the "WE" level of your life by exploring the five components that make up Life's Cosmic Equation. Through it, you will discover how you are connected to everyone and everything in the world. You are a part of something big and significant.

The idea of creating Life's Cosmic Equation was inspired by Albert Einstein and his theory of relativity. What if life itself could be broken down into a simple equation? After months of research, brainstorming, weekly recorded sessions, and strategic outlining, we were determined to come up with a simple and effective method to define and organize the key learning principles of our work.

Like $E=MC^2$, Life's Cosmic Equation is a simple tool to help you wrap your arms around the many ways you are connected to people. It is based on fundamental principles that exist in the world and the universe. It represents the naturally occurring driving force that inspires each of us to explore and discover all of life's potential.

There are five elements that make up Life's Cosmic Equation. On one side of the equation the three elements of Creative Power, Receptive Choice, and Faith are added together. Creative Power is the spark of energy and self-manifestation that exists in all things in the universe. Everything has a unique purpose for existing and contributing. Receptive Choice describes the relationship all things have to one another. All things exist in unity with something else. Faith represents the unknown destiny that lies within each of us to create a world of greater complexity.

*"Wisdom is knowing the right path to take . . .
integrity is taking it."*

M.H. Mckee

After being added together, the first three elements are multiplied by the fourth dimension of the universe known as Time. Time represents the combination of past, present, and future, all of which contribute to the final destiny of life's journey. The four elements combine to equal the composite of Life's Cosmic Legacy or the story of what you did and who you touched along the way. Now let's take a closer look at each of these elements individually and see how they provide insights into the direction and meaning of life.

WE ARE CONNECTED TO EVERYONE AND EVERYTHING IN THE WORLD

Your Cosmic Legacy:
Duane's the Tale of Two Lives with Two Wives

"To be or not to be, that is the question."

William Shakespeare

Dance with the Elephant: Life's Cosmic Equation

Here I am writing down my thoughts on the page. For more than a year I have dedicated my life to exploring the dynamics of human manifestation, unity, and transformation. What was a dream to write a single volume has now transformed into a vade mecum and what will be the supporting trilogy. I would have never given credence to such an undertaking back when I first got married twenty-five years ago and the sixteen tons of life experience that took place in between.

I think the first time I can remember someone using the phrase the elephant in the room was during some group counseling sessions I participated in when I was going through my divorce. For me, at the time, the elephant stood for the fact that my wife, after two children together, twelve years of marriage, and five years of courtship before that, decided to come out of the closet and dump me for her girlfriend on the softball team. So for me, the elephant was my story of personal loss and anguish. It took me over three years to finally be able to talk about this elephant without trying to run and hide.

I believe each of us at birth is given an apple seed to plant in life. In addition to the genetics of our parental lineage and the culture of our environment, this unique apple seed is an exact image of personal character, genius, calling, soul, fate, and destiny. In unity with the apple seed is an inner spirit or inspiring force that is meant to guide us through life. This attending spirit is present in our unconscious, cares about us, it protects us, and it takes an active interest in what we do in life. The apple seed represents everything we are meant to be in life. Our inner attending spirit loves us and brings guiding providence to our growth as an apple tree.

The success or failure of any relationship certainly is based on the four pillars that were introduced in the previous chapter: respect, trust, desire for growth, and confidentiality. In addition, I believe there are three common threads that tie two people together: their genetic temperament, their cultural personality, and their apple seed of character. Having studied and taught personality profiling throughout my career, I have been always fascinated by how likes and opposites sometimes attract and repel one another. I believe compatibility based on temperament and personality are the "make it or break it" in a relationship, but it's the apple seed of character that determines the difference between average and great partnerships.

I met my first wife when I was a junior in high school. Her folks had a cabin on the same lake where my grandparents lived. As kids growing up, we passed by each other many times on weekends while fishing, boating and water skiing, but we never paid much attention to each other. She was two years younger, and it wasn't until the summer when she magically filled out the top half of her bikini that my testosterone kicked in and added her to the list of ladies on my dating radar screen.

The two of us dated off and on over a five-year period. During this time, we both saw other people. But for every one new guy she dated, I probably had three or four girls on my list. At one time, I had seven different girls in seven different cities in my little black book. It was after our trip to Seattle, on a motorcycle together, that I decided to ask her to marry me. I was actually afraid I was going to lose her to another guy, and I felt it was time to end my playboy ways and settle down to raise a family.

We both grew up in blue-collar suburbs of Minneapolis and St. Paul, Minnesota. Our families both had ties to a strong German heritage. We were both excellent athletes in high school, and we shared a common competitive spirit. There was definitely an organic, physical attraction between us, now in retrospect, at least there was for me.

My first wife grew up in a family strongly affected by alcohol and divorce. *Jesus Christ, Superstar* was a popular Broadway play at the time. As I look back on it, I went into the marriage thinking I could be my wife's "superstar savior" from all the turmoil at home. I even thought I could rescue her entire family from all the alcoholic disfunction and codependency. Although my intentions were good, I was grossly naive and had no idea what I was truly facing and the impact it would have on my marriage.

I would rate our twelve years of marriage together as being above average overall. After I graduated from college, we moved to northern Minnesota where there was a greater chance of me finding a job in forestry. After a series of temporary jobs and relocations, we eventually progressed to become a middle-class couple with a home, two cars, a boat, a canoe, two lovely sons, two dogs, and a cat. We both were active in the community, had many friends, and maintained strong connections with distant family members. But, in looking back, there was always a level of tension between us. Early on, I thought it was just the competitive spirit between us. Now I know it was something more.

The two apple trees of life that represented our two lives had a number of branches that were definitely growing in opposite directions. One of my personal mottos has been "sixteen tons of life experience." The sixteen tons represent the sixteen different careers I have had. I'm sure my first wife would have much preferred for me to find an eight-to-five job, Monday through Friday, with great benefits and lots of vacation. She would have preferred my choosing a single career that I would continue in until retirement. Instead, during the seventeen years we were together, I went from: grease monkey to rock star, sheetrock sander to forester, creamery worker to county agent, and drywall distributor to college administrator. The straw that broke the camels back of our relationship came when I suggested moving to St. Cloud, Minnesota, in pursuit of my developing passion and a new career in computers.

I believe there were many things that prompted my ex-wife to come out of the closet when she did and to seek out a relationship with another woman. Although it took me twenty-five years after the fact to truly realize it, I believe that her inner spirit, her guiding force, included a stronger connection to women than it did to men. I honestly believe that had she grown up in a different family situation, outside the constraint of her domineering alcoholic father, she would have openly expressed her sexual preference much earlier in life. In looking back, I can remember a girlfriend she had during her high school years that played softball and ran track with her. I recall very vividly the emotional twinge I felt in observing their relationship together. There was a magic there, a chemistry, that under different circumstances could have easily developed into more than just being fellow teammates.

As I look back on the divorce and the pain and suffering it caused for so many people, I find myself dancing with the yin and yang of life and the capacity for the human brain to rationalize almost anything. Reflecting on the yin of my story, a part of me still has a lesbian-divorce-knife deeply penetrating in my side. A knife that inflicts piercing emotional pain any time I decide to mentally twist and turn it. I will always regret the torment and suffering my two sons had to endure. The divorce was bad enough, but the idea of my two sons being raised in an openly lesbian home, being chastised daily in school by kids mirroring the values of their conservative iron-range parents, just the thought breaks my heart to this day. My only hope is that my sons have or will someday forgive me for the choices I made. When I shift my conscious mind to the yang of this story, however, the fact is my two boys grew up in a home where they were loved and supported by their mother and her partner. On weekends whenever possible, during holidays, and every summer, they had a father and a step-mother who loved and cared for them dearly. Was it perfect? Was it ideal? Hell no! But whose life is? And who am I to think I can determine the journey and destiny of my children's apple seeds and the destiny of their spiritual guides? I will always love and I take great pride in my first two sons and the direction in life they have chosen for themselves. I also wish the very best for my ex-wife and her partner. I am happy to see that our society continues to evolve in a direction of equal rights for the gay community.

Was this a path in life I would have chosen for myself? Was this an outcome that my ex-wife would have predicted when she first married me? Would either of us have decided to bring our two sons into the world, had we known the direction our lives were headed? If life was simply based on human temperament and socially determined personality, the answer to these questions would be unequivocally no. But as it all relates to my life journey, guided by my personal inner spirit, the tree that grew from my apple seed included branches that were meant to reach out in new directions, different from the life I led with my first wife. The pain and suffering I experienced through the separation and divorce was meant to shake me up and challenge my way of thinking about myself. I have come to the realization that it is the unexpected and the surprises in my life that will often change the course, providing a new direction and target for my final destiny.

Don likes to talk about the drama and trauma of life, a Western version of the Chinese yin and yang philosophy. My divorce was the most traumatic event in my entire life. I would call it my life's most significant emotional event. It brought about an immediate end to who I thought I was, who I was supposed to be, and where my life was destined to take me. It blew me apart and required months of counseling and years of group therapy. It took three long years before I started to put the pieces back together again.

Now let me shift forward twenty-five years and take advantage of our ability to look back in time. The divorce forced me to shift my way of thinking about the world. On a canvas that was previously painted either totally black or totally white, I was given the opportunity to see shades of grey for the first time. The trauma that shook me to the core and destroyed most of my values and dreams became the launchpad to a different way of looking at life. The grief and suffering brought me to a new way of understanding and appreciating the gift that allowed my apple tree to grow branches in new directions. For the first time in my life, I read books because I wanted to. I listened to every self-help tape I could get my hands on. As a result, I set goals and created a new path that would bring reborn meaning and purpose to my life.

A sign that things were beginning to turn around took place late in 1988. As I recall, I was listening to a self-help tape by Tony Robbins when I wrote down twenty-two goals for myself and over the next five years I successfully accomplished every one of them. A number of them that I still remember included meet a woman whom I would love and cherish, start my own training company, take a trip to Germany, and publish a family history book.

I met Bette Lou in December 1989 and we started dating during the spring of 1990, just about the same time both of our divorces were being finalized. Bette was a breath of fresh air. On our first date, I discovered that she was a 4H kid extraordinaire and she found out I was a past county agent. For those of you who don't know anything about the Ag Extension Service, the discovery Bette and I made during our first time together was like spreading freshly churned butter on a slice of hot homemade bread that just came out of the oven. Mmmm… mouth-watering delicious!

My tale of two wives story is kind of like the caterpillar who has to die in the cocoon before it emerges reborn as a butterfly. My Cosmic Legacy journey with Bette has been like a butterfly learning to fly for the first time. Our unified creative power has reinvented my life in every direction. She sees strength in my diversity and encourages my future exploration into the unknown. Where my ex-wife was a great match with my physical being, Bette feeds all aspects of my mind, body, and spirit. It's as though my apple tree of life discovered a new source of more intense sunlight, richer soil nutrients, and a bottomless reservoir of water to draw upon. The list of gifts Bette and I have been blessed with over the past twenty years is almost infinite. The two children we created and nurtured together are the greatest example of our unified creative power. Our apple trees grow well together and the fruit we bear is plentiful, bringing meaning and purpose to our relationship and to the world.

My story here isn't about judgment or the need to choose right from wrong. It's about planting your apple seed in rich soil, open sunlight, and plentiful moisture. It's about letting go and allowing your inner spirit to help and guide you both in good times and bad. It's about connecting with people who feed you and whom you feed. It's about having the strength and courage to know when to change your direction. My cosmic legacy will be determined by the stories I created in the hearts of the people I touched and loved in life. The same will be true for you.

What
Are
Your
Reflections
on
Life?

Creative Power

"Every star and its solar system is exclusive and totally unique unto itself. Yet the life cycle of a solar system is the unity all things have with one another. You are just as unique and yet connected to everyone else on the planet."

Duane Kuss

Dance with the Elephant: Life's Cosmic Equation

CREATIVE POWER
THE FIRST PART OF LIFE'S COSMIC EQUATION

$$\left(\text{Creative Power} + \text{Receptive Choice} + \text{Faith} \right) \times \text{Time} = \text{Your Cosmic Legacy}$$

On a personal level, Creative Power is the AWESOME energy source within you. When it is completely understood, utilized, and acted upon, it will provide infinite capacity to fully realize your dreams and reach your destiny!

So what is the source of this Creative Power and from where did it come?

To find the answer to this question, all you have to do is look into the sky on a clear night. Did you know that on any given night, a star is being born? Since the beginning of time, there has been a creative force in the universe that **changes simple things into more complex ones.** This force is demonstrated on the cosmic level when clouds of hydrogen and helium gas fuse together to form stars. (See image of Eagle Nebula on page 46).

The birth, life, and death of a star can provide great insights into better understanding the role of Creative Power in the universe. From the moment of birth, a star has a cosmic creative energy and purpose manifested within it. Every star and its solar system is exclusive and unique unto itself. It was born with a given size, a certain brightness, a given life span, and most important, a relationship with the other objects that orbit it. These objects include asteroids, comets, planets, and sometimes even other stars. No two stellar systems are alike.

"Excellence is never an accident. It is always the result of high intention, sincere effort, and intelligent execution; it represents the wise choice of many alternatives - choice, not chance, determine your destiny."

Aristotle

A star lives to shine bright, providing energy and gravity to its solar system. During its lifetime, important creative work is going on in the nuclear belly of the star. The simple elements of hydrogen and helium are being converted into more complex elements like nitrogen, oxygen, and carbon. It is during the final moments that precede the death of a star that most of the simple to complex element conversion takes place. In the grand finale, a star leaves its own cosmic legacy when it explodes in a supernova and hurls its heavier elements and precious metals back into the galaxy, providing the seeds for new stars to be born and the opportunity for the entire cycle to begin again.

Another important aspect to Creative Power that is observable in the life cycle of a solar system is **the unity all things have with one another**. Nothing in the universe exists unto itself. Everything is associated and has a relationship with something else. Hydrogen and helium combine to make up the nuclear energy needed to form a star. The explosive supernova death of a star creates the heavier elements of carbon, iron, nitrogen, and oxygen. Galactic clouds of heavier elements are pulled together by the gravitational force of other stars to form comets, asteroids, and planets. Planets that orbit at the right distance from the light and heat energy of their parent star can create conditions that encourage geological formations, bodies of water, chemical reactions, and eventually life itself. Yes, you are made of stardust, and you are connected in unity with everything and everyone around you.

The same Creative Power that gives form and meaning to the night sky exists within you. Your journey to discovering and exploring your Creative Power can provide you a shortcut to understanding your true destiny. It will become a source of daily energy, vibrance, joy, and exhilaration that brings greater purpose and meaning to your life.

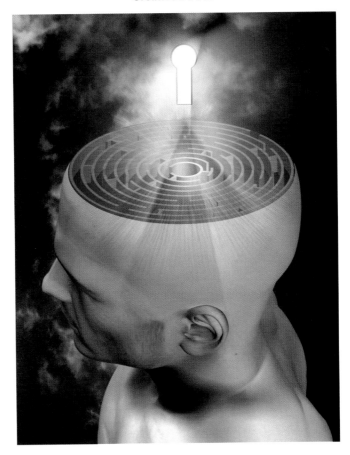

"Hope is a waking dream."

Aristotle

Dance with the Elephant: Life's Cosmic Equation

Do you know what your Creative Power is?

Unfortunately, most people have never thought of even asking the question. Look around you. How many people do you know that have allowed the social and cultural influences of family, friends, and society to control their beliefs and direction in life? They are blind to the inborn Creative Power of the universe and the joyful purpose it can bring to life. Most people have turned away from the Creative Power they felt sometime during their youth or maybe never really got acquainted with it.

So let's take a quick journey back in time to the days when you were between the ages of eight and twelve years old. Take out a sheet of paper and write down the answers to the following questions. Continue reading only after you have written down at least six ideas that pop into your head when you look into your past.

- What excited you back then?
- What hobbies or interests did you have?
- Who were your favorite heroes and villains?
- What were your favorite classes in school?
- What did you want to be "when you grew up"?
- Was there anything you did that was both challenging and rewarding at the same time?
- What kind of people or things did you take most delight in?
- What did you daydream about?
- What in life did you find most gratifying?
- If money wasn't a concern, what would you have done with your life?

These questions are important because they allow you to reflect and remember a time when your dreams, imagination, and creative energy was most likely at their apex. You still have the capacity to tap back into this awesome Creative Power.

"Be of good cheer. Do not think of today's failures, but of the success that may come tomorrow. You have set yourselves a difficult task, but you will succeed if you persevere, and you will find a joy in overcoming obstacles. Remember, no effort that we make to attain something beautiful is ever lost."

Helen Keller

You are unique, different, and special. In fact, like each of the lone stars in the sky, there is no one exactly like you in the entire universe. You alone bring to this world the perfect combination of gifts, talents, knowledge, body, and spirit. Your Creative Power is your personal treasure chest waiting to be opened, explored, and discovered. It is your purpose and destiny to apply your Creative Power in this world to make an extraordinary contribution for yourself, your family, your community, your country, your world, and your universe. It is the people you touch during the journey in life that makes the difference in what will be your legacy.

Discovering your Creative Power is your link and connection to everyone and everything around you. It's the spark that lights the fire within you every day to meet life's challenges and opportunities. No one can truly tell you what your Creative Power is. It's something that only you can discover and nurture within yourself. It can be as simple as truly enjoying the smell of flowers in a garden or as complex as the pursuit of some new theory of relativity in the universe. You personally have a role to play and a story to contribute that will make a difference. There is a self-manifestation, a purpose, a driving force that burns within you. You are meant to tap into your Creative Power and let it guide you to reaching your destiny. Call it what you like: Life's purpose, its destiny, your personal passions, or life's precious gifts. All of these are describing the same universal source, your Creative Power.

Creative Power: Duane's Story of
with a Little Help from My Friends

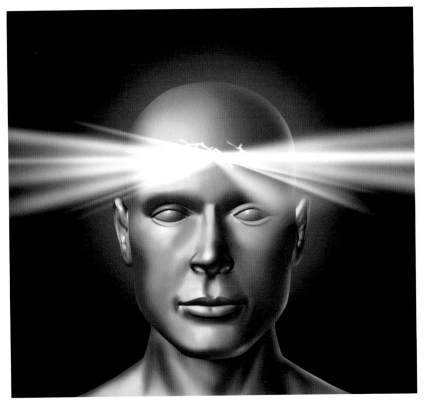

"Creative Power is the unique energy source within you. When identified, understood, utilized and acted upon, it will provide you infinite capacity to fully realize your dreams and reach your final destiny!"

Duane Kuss & Don Calhoun

Duane & Bette

My wife Bette and I live out in the country in Central Minnesota on a small body of water called Hermit Lake. Our English Tudor home sits high on a hill overlooking the quiet piece of water. The home has floor-to-ceiling windows that provide great views of nature, sunsets, and the changing seasons.

In the center of the house, on the main floor, there is a music room where Bette daily runs her fingers across the ebony and ivory. She is always preparing for one of her weekly performances at a church, school, or community festival. You might also find her working with one of her students, gladly passing along her talent, wisdom, and greatest passion.

Bette grew up as the youngest of three kids on a farm in South Central Minnesota. She attended a country church school and helped her mom and dad raise thousands of egg-laying chickens on their farm. While growing up, Bette was never very good at physical activity or sports; in fact, most would judge her to be clumsy and uncoordinated. She struggled and had to work harder than most to keep her grades up as she moved from the country school to the local high school. Growing up practically all alone on the farm gave Bette little experience with making friends and understanding the cruel realities of teenage cliques and social groups. In many ways, Bette was an outcast and never really fit in with her classmates during her high school years.

But there was one thing that Bette learned how to do early in life, which set her apart from the rest. Once a week, her mother would drive her fifty miles round trip to meet privately with her piano teacher. After many years of piano lessons and piano recitals, she cultivated her natural talent and gift for music. Bette

"*Go confidently in the direction of your dreams.
Live the life you have imagined.*"

Henry David Thoreau

can sit down at the piano and make magical heavenly sounds on the keys. She has touched thousands of people with her music and she truly understands the gift of her Creative Power and how it has led to her destiny and greatest contribution in life.

This story is important because it illustrates that each of us has a unique creative power. What we also learned was that we need others to help us in our journey. Bette had two important people who connected with her and greatly influenced her journey. Reflecting back on your life, who has been influential in helping you grow in understanding and discovering your Creative Power?

Creative Power:
Don's Story of Edie and Elton

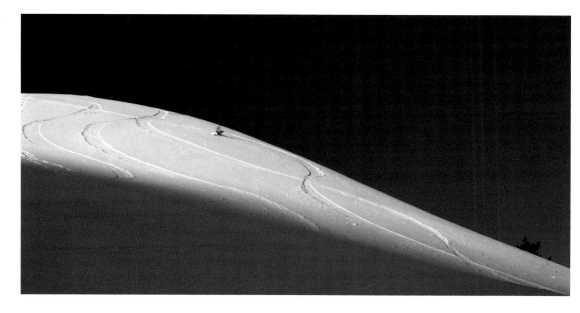

*"The mind is its own place,
and in itself can make a heaven of hell,
a hell of heaven."*

John Milton

Don's Golden Ticket

I was only five, and had just graduated from kindergarten and was driving home with my mother, Edie. I remember asking my mother, "Why are you driving through the stop signs, Mommy?" Later, when we arrived at home, Mom parked the car in the garage and entered the house through a back door that led to a small add-on bedroom. My mother promptly hit the bedroom floor like a sack of potatoes and started convulsing with a grand-mal seizure. I had never witnessed an event like this before. Watching my mother lie on the ground, twisting, turning, and wailing was forever burned into my brain. A half century later, the feelings of helplessness and confusion watching my mother in pain are still vivid and real.

My strong connection to music began on Wednesday, October 10, 1979, in Northrop Auditorium on the campus of the University of Minnesota in Minneapolis. I can still vividly remember the energy and anticipation that evening: it was simply electric! As the house lights went down, some 4,800 fans broke into a thunderous roar as Elton John took the stage, and to my surprise, I was all alone. It was just Elton, his piano, and a single spotlight that launched that magical night into flight. That evening three college friends and I experienced the awesome Creative Power of Elton John's music. My immediate reaction to the night included feelings of happiness, euphoria, and joy. All of this was a welcome respite from a very difficult and traumatic time in my life.

Years earlier, after her seizure, my mother was diagnosed with brain cancer. The family doctor gave my mother only three months to live following a very difficult

"Nothing can stop the person with the right mental attitude from achieving their goal; nothing on earth can help the individual with the wrong mental attitude."

Thomas Jefferson

brain surgery. Against all odds, my mother survived not only months but years. It wasn't until my junior year in high school that my mother underwent a second brain surgery and another hellish round of chemotherapy and radiation treatments. But the toll of the grapefruit-sized brain tumor and the multiple surgeries had left my mother blind and in need of constant care.

For the most part, I never knew what it was like to have a normal mother. Early on, I grew up having to be my mother's eyes and daily caregiver. But I never looked at it that way. For myself, she was a mom just like any other mom. She was very strong mentally and carried herself with a quiet dignity. Throughout her struggles, she never complained and always exemplified an attitude of gratitude. She is and will always be my greatest hero.

The Elton John concert took place during a time that the health of my mother was once again seriously deteriorating. Her seizures were coming so often that she had to be hospitalized. She was given a mouth guard to prevent her from biting her own tongue. Eventually, she fell into a coma. I was a college junior at Saint John's University. Witnessing my mother's final weeks of suffering brought intense feelings of pain, isolation, and helplessness. It was impossible for me to try to concentrate on my studies. Things got so bad that I seriously considered dropping out of college. It was a difficult time for me, trying to adhere to the gracious standards of my dying mother and yet torn apart by all the pain and misery she had to endure. It just wasn't fair. In fact, it "*sucked*!"

Before the concert on that October 1979 night, I had been an Elton John fan for some time. After that night, however, my loyalty became almost fanatical. Somehow, the experience of that evening tapped into my Creative Power and hardwired a link between music and positive emotions within myself. As crazy as it

*"To see a world in a grain of sand
And a heaven in a wild flower,
Hold infinity in the palm of your hand
And eternity in an hour."*

William Blake

may sound, music, especially Elton's, became my tool for escaping anxiety and discovering personal freedom. Music became emotionally hardwired into my spiritual psyche to connect me with the feelings of joy, bliss, and euphoria. From that day forward, whenever I have felt down or depressed, I just plug in to my favorite tunes, and it changes my mood almost instantaneously. Within moments, my mind is transported to a magical place: one of positive energy, universal power, and divine purpose.

Unlike Bette's Creative Power story referenced earlier in this chapter, I was not blessed with the ability to read music, sing, or play a musical instrument; however, I connected to a different musical Creative Power linked to the music other people create, better known as a musicologist. Over the years I have acquired a large collection of music and an interest in a wide variety of genres. I have leveraged my passion and delight in music by being a disc jockey in college and at weddings. In more recent years, I have acted as my own musical producer by distributing an annual "CalRock" favorite songs CD to family, friends, and associates. I continually explore the music world, looking for new and interesting music, sweet-sounding melodies that capture my heart and soul. Live concerts are the ultimate high for me. Since that first concert in 1979, I have attended a total of eighteen Elton John live performances. I also attend the live shows of many other music artists. And to think that all of this ties back to that fateful night when Elton sat down at his piano and sang "Rocket Man" with me attentively listening in the audience, the moment that illuminated my Creative Power and branded my musical soul forever.

When you consider what Bette's piano playing did for her and what Elton John's music did for me, it's the goal of this book to encourage, guide, and assist you in discovering or reaffirming your Creative Power. What insights did you get from

"It is obvious that we can no more explain a passion to a person who has never experienced it than we can explain light to the blind."

T. S. Eliot

the answers you wrote down about your dreams and interests when you were growing up?

This story is important because it illustrates that each of us has traumatic events in our life that require us to dig deeper and find meaning and purpose in order to move forward. You need to find and connect with your Creative Power to give you strength. What you connect with will be unique to you. Mine is music. Duane's is exploration and science. What is yours?

Learn more about Creative Power at DancewiththeElephant.org

*"There are no constraints on the human mind,
no walls around the human spirit, no barriers to
our progress except those we ourselves erect."*

Ronald Reagan

Creative Power Unleashed: Think back to a special time during your childhood where you felt extremely connected to your family or friends. This was a time that you felt totally alive, full of energy, and truly in the moment. It may be helpful for you to think of watching your favorite childhood movie, dancing or singing to a memorable song, or visiting a favorite place. Think of a time where you said to yourself, "This is what I must do," "This is what I've got to have," and "This is who I am!" Reflect back on this event and ponder the following questions:

As a kid, who or what did you want to be when you grew up?

What feelings of joy, excitement, love, and connection do you remember from your experience?

What was going on in your life at the time? How did the experience make you feel about your strengths, talents, self-worth, and connection with others?

What did you learn from this experience?

How would you have completed this sentence as a teenager, "My destiny, my calling and my reason for being alive in this world is to…"?

What was the plot of your story? Who were you meant to be?

Why were you born into the world?

Creative Power Inhibited: Think back to a traumatic moment in your childhood where you felt embarrassed, shameful, guilty, or emotional pain that was caused by your family or friends. This was a time that you were full of anxiety, fear, disconnect, or emotional insecurities. It may be helpful for to you to think about watching a scary movie, an embarrassing sporting performance, or a place you hated to go. Reflect back on this event and ponder the following questions:

How did you internalize your feelings from this event? Did you just try to block it out of your mind? Did you blame someone else?

Try to grow deeper into the protection mechanisms you may have used and understand how this event disconnected you from your dreams, creative energy, and personal calling in life.

What has been the emotional cost of this traumatic event in your life?

In looking back, are there angry resentments or overwhelming longings that come to mind?

What is one thing that you could do today, or this week, to reconnect with these difficult childhood moments and bring closure, self-respect, and growth back to who you are now?

Creative Power Understood: The purpose of reflecting back and remembering both positive and negative experiences is to help you rediscover why and how you became who you are today. Your internal dialogue should be directed toward your ability to learn and grow as an individual, irrespective of your past choices and your journey up to now. You should endeavor to reconnect with your dreams, creative energy, and passion for life. Your emotional language should be in harmony with your calling, your character, and your unique purpose for being you. Here are some other creative power questions for further exploration:

What brings you joy and happiness? What gets you really excited to be alive?

What three things are you most proud of in your life today?

What do you do that you become so involved with that time seems to stop or time seems to fly by?

If you were to read your life backward, whose story would you be telling? Your genes? Your ancestry? Your trauma? Your parents? Your social norms?

How would you complete the phrase, "I was born to…"?

What are you best at? Singing? Dancing? Writing? Drawing or painting? Laughing? Inventing?

What would you give to live a life that was full of those positive feelings and energy?

What is one thing that you could do today, or this week, to reconnect with your dreams, energy, and passion?

Receptive Choice

*"The human brain is a complex organ
with the wonderful power of enabling man
to find reasons for continuing to believe
whatever it is that he wants to believe."*

Voltaire

RECEPTIVE CHOICE
THE SECOND PART OF LIFE'S COSMIC EQUATION

$$\left(\text{Creative Power} + \text{Receptive Choice} + \text{Faith} \right) \times \text{Time} = \text{Your Cosmic Legacy}$$

Earlier in this book, when defining the term Creative Power, we posed the old cliche every kid was asked: "What do you want to be when you grow up?" Now, as we move on to the second component of Life's Cosmic Equation, Receptive Choice, the question is again relevant. Did you grow up choosing to be what you really wanted? Through Receptive Choice you are given the ability to choose and filter how you perceive the world around you. You also have the capability of selecting who and how you communicate with others. You have the capacity to determine the level of influence any given person, group, or event has on the direction of your life.

But there's another paradox of humanity involved here. Even though you and everyone else is given the gift of Receptive Choice at birth, most of the choices made during life are actually dictated and controlled by the socioeconomic system in which you live. Social norms and culture are the driving forces that define you. They determine how you act and react in your family, community, and country. You abide by the rules and guidelines of the times based on your geographic location. Instead of making conscious and purposeful Receptive Choices, most people are puppets of their environment, and in the big picture of a constantly evolving humanity, very few individuals break free from the cultural chains that bind them.

The Road Not Taken

Two roads diverged in a yellow wood,
And sorry I could not travel both
And be one traveler, long I stood
And looked down one as far as I could
To where it bent in the undergrowth;

Then took the other, as just as fair,
And having perhaps the better claim,
Because it was grassy and wanted wear;
Though as for that the passing there
Had worn them really about the same,

And both that morning equally lay
In leaves no step had trodden black.
Oh, I kept the first for another day!
Yet knowing how ways leads on to way,
I doubted if I should ever come back.

I shall be telling this with a sigh
Somewhere ages and ages hence:
Two roads diverged in a wood, and I -
I took the one less traveled by,
And that has made all the difference.

Robert Frost

In 1916, author and poet Robert Frost detailed our reality to choose in his beautiful poem "The Road Not Taken." You have been given the gift of Receptive Choice. You can control your life's journey, your perceptions, and for that matter, your reality. Receptive Choice has been a part of human history for centuries, contemplated and illustrated by our great philosophers, theologians, historians, and storytellers.

"I think, therefore I am."
René Descartes, a seventeen-century French philosopher

"We become what we think about."
William James, American psychologist and philosopher

There is a famous Native American parable where the tribal chief is telling a story to his grandson about two wolves who lived in the wild. The one wolf represented everything that is good in the world: the warm sun in summer and the hot wood fire in the winter; the emotions of joy, euphoria, happiness, hope, and love. The other wolf represented all that is bad in the world: the cold freezing temperatures of winter and the pounding destructive winds of a summer tornado; the emotions of evil, pain, greed, despair, and hate.

The chief continued his story by describing the two wolves in a great battle against each other, ripping and tearing at each other's throats. He went on to describe how the wolves represent the battle that goes on with every human being, a battle that his grandson would someday wage within himself. The grandson was totally captured by the story and in a moment of desperation pleaded with the chief, "But Grandfather, which of the wolves will win inside me?" And the chief slowly kneeled down and looked directly into the eyes of his grandson and softly spoke, "The wolf that gets fed."

"It is not for me to judge another man's life.
I must judge, I must choose, I must spurn, purely for myself.
For myself, alone."

Hermann Hesse

The truth is Receptive Choice is your gift and responsibility, not someone else's. Receptive Choice is really the golden ticket, the precious key, to understanding how to take total control and responsibility of your life. Receptive Choice means you're going to be open and available to your creative energy. You will consciously work to understand, nurture, and develop yourself, so you can maximize your unique journey in the universe. You will learn to accept responsibility for your choices and purpose in life. Receptive Choice is understanding that you control the steering wheel, brakes, and gas pedal of your life.

Since life began as we know it, all living organisms have been a part of the cosmic law of unity. Everything exists in unity with something else. Nothing lives in total isolation or independence. All living things are constantly evolving in a continuous dance with similar species, toward greater complexity and higher forms of interaction. This activity has been studied and documented by the science community. Even simple cells have social and cosmic interaction. We know organic living cells, birds, fish, mammals all show signs of interaction, repelling, and attraction. We may not think they are given Receptive Choice, but they fully demonstrate, through their capacity of survival, the ability to adapt and evolve through space and time.

Another example in today's society where our disconnect with Receptive Choice is blatantly evident can be seen by those who have leadership roles. Are you the owner of a business, a manager of a company, or a coach of a Little League team? When something goes wrong or something happens that wasn't planned, who is responsible? Isn't it always somebody else's fault? Do you ever see a team member or coworker step up to the plate and say, "I did it! I screwed up! I am responsible." No, most of the time blame is placed on somebody or something else. Shame, blame, and guilt are always reflected on somebody other than the party who was truly responsible.

Receptive Choice:
Don's Story of the Ultimate Echo Effect

"Receptive Choice empowers you to discover the magical path in life, in perfect harmony with your Creative Power. It will set you free from the shackles of judgment by others and it will lead you to beautiful horizons on your unique and personal legacy journey."

Duane Kuss & Don Calhoun

I was the extremely shy kid in the neighborhood, especially when it came to interacting with the opposite sex. I didn't exhibit a lot of confidence in myself and was very content to hide away in the shadows of daily life. I was blessed with very close male friends in my neighborhood, but that's as big as the social circle got.

In school, most kids didn't even realize I was in their class. I did my best to stay out of the limelight and to avoid anything that would bring attention to myself. But when I reached the tenth grade, that all was about to change. Tom Steinke, my electronics teacher, was destined to redirect my personal compass and path in life.

One fall day, Mr. Steinke approached me during his electronics class and asked me to please stay after for a moment. Although I, in most subjects in school, was by no means an honor student, when it came to electronics, it just seemed to come easy for me. I didn't even have to study much to understand the basics and fundamental concepts of electricity. Mr. Steinke, or more fondly remembered now as Tom, took me into a small room attached to the electronics lab and had me sit down in a chair. Tom found his own chair and sat down right in front of me so that he could look at me eye to eye.

"Don," he asked, "what are you planning on doing with your life?"

I had no idea what the hell he was talking about. As a knee-jerk reaction I just shrugged my shoulders and gently shook my head left to right, totally bewildered.

"Seriously, Don, what are you going to do with your life, now and after high school?" asked Tom.

*"You can search throughout the entire universe
for someone who is more deserving of your love
and affection than you are yourself, and that
person is not to be found anywhere. You, yourself,
as much as anybody in the entire universe,
deserves your love and affection."*

Gautama Buddha

I was uncomfortably squirming now. The pressure was on; I had to come up with something. "Well, I guess I'd like to waterski."

Tom's face now became even more stern. "Don, I just don't think waterskiing is going to cut it. You frustrate the living hell out of me, son. You are very bright! You don't even have to study to get a B in my class. Electronics is not an easy subject, but you get it without even trying. You need to think bigger. Think of yourself as a ship out in the ocean. If you don't have a rudder to provide you with direction, your ship will be at the mercy of the wind and the waves. You will be just cast about, to and fro. You will never end up at any meaningful destination. You need a port of call, a direction that you want to sail. Don, you will even have the ability to change course along the way, but you need to pick somewhere, anywhere to sail toward."

It was this ten minute, heart-to-heart talk that had more impact on my life than any single event before or after. Somehow, shortly after that talk, I realized at the tender age of fifteen that I had the opportunity to change the direction of my life. I realized that I did not have to hide in the shadows, with zero direction or ambition. It was clear I had the capacity, within myself, to change. Now the question was if I had the courage to make it happen. The fear of failure and the insecurities of the past were enormous. Thank goodness, I determined that the risk of doing nothing was far greater than the risk of failing.

After that day, I made a simple choice to do everything I hated or feared. I made the decision to throw my emotional cork and insecurity to the wind. I immediately began simple steps to move forward on my journey. I signed up for speech, became a lector at church, actively sought out new friends, joined in on new activities, and actually started studying! I was determined to set sail on a new life of adventure. For the first time, I had a purpose to my life. I really had no idea where I wanted to go. I just knew that selecting any place was better than no place at all. The act of

*"We have the power to choose our perception.
We can look to the obvious or apparent, or try
to understand the meaning below the surface.
We can find the good or bad in any event; our
focus is within our control."*

Don Calhoun

throwing caution to the wind and facing fears head-on proved to be exhilarating. I knew there was no way my life was ever going to be the same. The echo effect of Tom's act of kindness that day has been profound. A person may never know if and when an act of caring, listening, and sharing will leave a lasting effect on someone's life. We are all faced with choices every day. We can choose to help or we can avoid others. We have the capacity to help a friend in need, save a marriage, prevent a suicide, or give meaning and purpose to a friend. Tom had that same choice, and he chose to try to help a young man "blowing in the wind." His actions proved to be a defining moment in my life. The reality is that most of us will never know the echo effect of our actions. But that does not mean we should not act.

I had the fortune to meet with Tom just weeks before he passed away. When the two of us talked, Tom had no recollection of our conversation when I was back in high school. I was blessed with the opportunity to share with Tom the powerful effect he had on my life. I am eternally grateful that he had the courage and conviction to care enough to intervene in my teenage life. Because he did, my life has never been the same.

Thomas J. Steinke
April 22, 1932
September 28, 2010

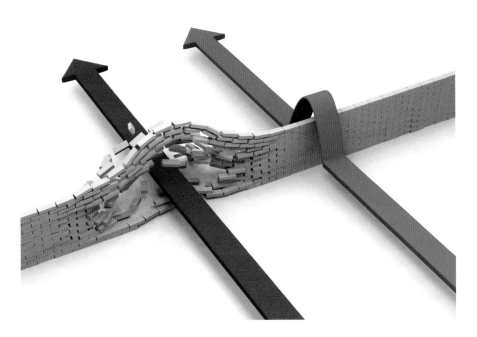

"I won't tell you that the world matters nothing, or the world's voice, or the voice of society. They matter a good deal. They matter far too much. But there are moments when one has to choose between living one's own life, fully, entirely, completely—or dragging out some false, shallow, degrading existence that the world in its hypocrisy demands. You have that moment. Choose!"

Oscar Wilde

This story is important because it illustrates that you are indeed connected to others. Just like Tom, you have the capacity to impact the lives of others in a significant way. You might never be fortunate enough, however, to learn when and how. As you look back on your life, do you remember any life-altering conversations? If so take a moment to seek the people who influenced you and let them know. You deserve to slow down enough to have more conversations that have substance and purpose. You have the ability to make new and more empowering choices. You have the ability to change your attitude, behavior, or beliefs. You just need to believe that it is possible. You actually have the power to plan out your choices in life! You can hone your ability to focus. You can keep fear, control, or excuses from limiting your growth.

Our perceptions naturally change over time.
The "echo effect" of any event can be truly life-changing if
we are brave enough to examine and learn from them!

Receptive Choice:
Duane's Uncommon Choice

"Rules and models destroy genius and art"

William Hazlitt

My mother-in-law Ruth's funeral was held at her country church just five miles north of Gibbon, Minnesota. It was a mid-December day when rain turned to snow and a thick layer of ice covered the church parking lot. Ruth had died a week earlier at her daughter Bette's home on Hermit Lake on December 7, 2012.

Bette and I had invited Ruth to come live with us back in July 2012. At the time, Ruth was living in a nursing home about five miles away from Bette and my home. Ruth now required full-time oxygen as well as special hospice care. Bette was the primary caregiver among her siblings and would visit Ruth almost every day, usually two to four hours at a time. It was actually I who first proposed the idea that Ruth should come live her final days with our family on Hermit Lake. When Ruth was posed with the question during one of Bette's visits, she immediately responded positively to the idea.

Now, it's very likely most people would consider Bette and I to be totally crazy to consider caring for the needs of a nintey-two-year-old woman who can't do anything for herself other than eat and drink what's placed in front of her. This would be a twenty-four-hour, seven-days-a-week care commitment that included preparing meals, assistance in and out of a wheelchair, sponge bathing, assistance onto and off of the commode, emptying the commode bucket, laundry services, and managing medications. In today's modern society and its mainstream values, there are very few people who would even consider the idea. Heck, Don himself asked me if I was "stark raving mad"? But after reconsidering, his next response was, "How beautiful a gift this would be for Bette and her mother."

The part of the story that most people wouldn't realize is the pressure that was placed on Bette and me for even looking into the possibility of having Ruth live with us. It was mind-boggling to consider all the issues that surfaced when it came to removing Ruth from the nursing home and bringing her to Hermit Lake to live her final days with family. Even Bette's siblings were up in arms over the

"*The past is already gone, the future is not yet here.
There's only one moment for you to live, and that is
the present moment.*"

Gautama Buddha

idea. In the end, the pressure placed on Bette and me to totally scuttle the idea was enormous. But here is where the concept of Receptive Choice came to bare. Bette and I had to make a choice as to what and whom we would listen. What did Ruth want and what was in her best interest during her final days of life?

Bette and I, against the opinions of health professionals, family, and friends, chose to bring Ruth home to live with us on Hermit Lake. Even though society as a whole threw up road blocks and predicted tales of horror, Bette and I chose to go the road less traveled and to follow our receptive choice to do what was right for Ruth. To all things there is a risk to be taken and a price to be paid. Your ability to recognize and activate your own receptive choice outside the social and cultural norms of society can empower you to move mountains.

Ruth's last four months were some of the most joyous and memorable she had in years. Her health improved, she was able to get out of her wheelchair and actively walk around the house with her walker. She had tea parties on the deck and "happy hour" under the ironwood tree. I built her a Facebook page that she daily interacted with, connecting her with relatives and friends she hadn't seen or heard from in years. She loved living with her grandchildren and being a part of their busy daily lives. She remained mentally and physically active until two days before she died. Bringing Ruth home to live on Hermit Lake was the right thing to do for Ruth, Bette, and myself. Family lovingly caring for family is the right thing to do, regardless what the patterns and norms of society might be at any given moment in time.

What Bette and I faced socially in bringing Ruth home to live with us is just a microcosm of what every human being faces each day in the cultural norms that surround them. In reality, the world around us, filled with all of its "thou shalts" and "thou shalt nots," is a part of a constantly evolving system of neurotic rules.

"As the winds and rain slowly erase the tangible aspects of our life, your major contribution to humanity will be measured by the stories you created in the hearts of the people you touched. There will be no moving van to haul your earthly possessions to the grave."

Don Calhoun

The best way to understand this is to look back one hundred years from today and think about what the cultural values and issues of the day were. Back then one most likely had to deal with things like where to tie up the horse or who was responsible for cleaning up the mess it left in the middle of the street. Imagine going back another one hundred years, or one thousand years? Examining the history of culture and values, it is easy to understand how societal norms have evolved over time. The same is true if you let your imagination go forward in time. Can you imagine five, ten, or even fifty years into the future at the exponential rate by which things are changing today? There is no question that our society will be different. The point here being that values, rules, norms are always changing. What was not allowed in the past may be fully accepted and supported in the near future.

In reality, your day-to-day life is highly influenced and controlled by cultural craziness. In order for you to successfully apply your Creative Power in the world, you will need to leverage your Receptive Choice to reject or accept constantly evolving social norms. When you learn to dance with the elephant, you'll have the freedom and power to choose what you'll be receptive to and what you'll totally ignore.

Ruth Grewe
December 24, 1919
December 7, 2012

Learn more about Receptive Choice at <u>DancewiththeElephant.org</u>

*"My grandfather once told me that there were two kinds
of people: Those who do the work, and those who take
the credit. He told me to try to be in the first group;
there was much less competition."*

Indira Gandhi

Receptive Choice Unleashed: Think back to an individual or cartoon character who was your hero and how he or she inspired you during your formative years. It may be helpful for you to remember your favorite movie actor, singer, writer, artist, or athlete. Did you have a favorite television show you enjoyed watching, a cartoon book series you read, or a particular author you felt a connection to? Reflect back on your heroes at the time and answer the following questions:

Why did they inspire you?

What was going on in your life at the time?

In addition to heroes, what other mentors did you have while growing up?

How did they make you feel about your strengths, self-worth, and connection with others?

What did you learn from them, and are they still a hero in your life today?

What positive choices did they make to empower their lives?

What is one thing that you could do today, or this week, that would reconnect you with this experience and help you make better choices in your life?

Receptive Choice Inhibited: Look back to your youth and think about those individuals or characters you considered to be complete hooligans or villains. These individuals represented everything you wanted to avoid and dissociate yourself with in life. They may have brought about feelings of fear, pain, anger, shame, or guilt. It may be helpful for to you to think about the worst person in your family or neighborhood or a public figure who was an embarrassment. It could also be a movie or cartoon character who would stir up feelings of fear and anxiety in you. Reflect back on these individuals and respond to the following questions:

Why did you have such negative feelings toward this individual?

Why do you think they were the way they were?

How did they make bad choices with their destiny?

What can you learn from their behavior to improve your life? How do their core values contrast to your own?

Based on the choices you have made since, did anything positive result from the hooligans of your past?

What is one thing that you could do today to move on from their negative influence?

Receptive Choice Understood: The purpose of reflecting back on your heroes and hooligans is to examine how people inspired and motivated you in a positive or a negative way. Ultimately, you have to take ownership of your life and your journey. Your choices should be made in harmony with your creative power and ultimate destiny. The following questions are meant to encourage you to explore the choices you make in life in relation to the influence of others:

Do your close friends and family support, encourage, motivate, and inspire you to be the best you can be?

Did you choose your career path on your own, based on your dreams and desires, or was it primarily influenced by the people and places you grew up with?

What about your education, hobbies, and activities? Do you feel you made the right choices based on your passions?

List three people within your work, church, or community whom you admire and whom you believe make good choices? How can you begin to learn from them?

Were your parents or siblings controlling? How did they influence your behavior positively or negatively?

What rules in your life make sense to you? What rules don't? What are your triggers for rebellion? Why? Do they make sense? Is your inner voice helpful or hurtful in your ability to make decisions?

Who are the people in your life who challenge you, support you, and feed you positively?

If money was no object, what would you do for the rest of your life?

Faith

*"Do not think that love in order to be genuine has
to be extraordinary. What we need is to love
without getting tired. Be faithful in small things
because it is in them that your strength lies."*

Mother Teresa

FAITH
THE THIRD PART OF LIFE'S COSMIC EQUATION

$$\left(\text{Creative Power} + \text{Receptive Choice} + \text{Faith} \right) \times \text{Time} = \text{Your Cosmic Legacy}$$

Faith is the third part of Life's Cosmic Equation. When added to Creative Power and Receptive Choice it makes up what is called the cosmic trinity. The cosmic trinity makes up the unifying creative force that joins together all things in the universe. Faith allows you to cope with the constant unknown part of daily life. No one knows what tomorrow will bring, yet through faith, we can survive and even thrive in the uncertainty. You can be fully connected to your passionate creative purpose and your reason for existing, but it is faith that bridges who you are today with the uncertain destiny of what you will become tomorrow.

One of the biggest reasons you need faith in your life was best described by Ernest Becker in his Pulitzer Prize–winning book, *The Denial of Death*. Becker describes in great detail how culture has evolved in human consciousness as the direct result of two predominant driving forces:

• the human need to avoid death

• the human need to pursue immortality

"Never give in. Never give in. Never, never, never,
never—in nothing, great or small, large or petty—never
give in, except to convictions of honor and good sense.
Never yield to force. Never yield to the apparently
overwhelming might of the enemy."

Winston Churchill

The terrifying reality that you and every person must face every day includes:

1. Yes, the cradle of life is death, and your life will culminate with this inevitable reality.

2. Not only will you die, but your death can come at any moment by accident or happenstance.

3. The meaning of your death will be no different from the roadkill you see along the highway.

Now, before your mind starts running for the hills in neurotic desperation, let's reference one of Becker's mentors, Soren Kierkegaard. Kierkegaard attempts to explain how we can deal with this overwhelming dilemma in human cultural evolution. He has his own formula for what he believes it means to be a human. He describes what he calls "the knight of faith."

This figure (the knight of faith) is the man who lives in faith, who has given over the meaning of life to his Creator, and who lives centered on the energies of his Maker. He accepts whatever happens in this visible dimension without complaint, lives his life as a duty, faces his death without qualm. No pettiness is so petty that it threatens his meanings; no task is too frightening to be beyond his courage. He is fully in the world on its terms and wholly beyond the world in his trust in the invisible dimension. He continues: As the knight of faith has no fear-of-life-and-death trip to lay onto others, he does not cause them to shrink back upon themselves, he does not coerce or manipulate them. The knight of faith, then, represents what we might call an ideal of mental health, the continuing openness of life out of the death throes of dread.

Cultivating an awareness and knowledge of your death can lead you to having faith

"*Courage is resistance to fear,*
mastery of fear—not
absence of fear."

Mark Twain

and trust in the sacred vitality of the universe. You can have faith in being a part of a big story, one that brings meaning and purpose to your life and one that will lead to your cosmic legacy in the form of power and wisdom, passed along to future generations.

Faith is the belief, deep within your being, a gut feeling, that you have the power to achieve a goal, deepen a relationship, or explain something that is not immediately provable. Faith is the reservoir of harnessed creative power and energy that provides meaning and purpose to our existence. Without faith in yourself, in others, or in a higher power, you will not fully achieve your Cosmic Legacy.

Faith needs to be applied at the three levels of human existence, the "Me," the "We," and the "What Will Be." Do you have faith in yourself? Are you committed to the relationships and the people who are closest to you in life? Do you have courage, determination, and strength to believe that the culmination of your relationships and experiences will bring purpose and fulfillment to your destiny and legacy?

Your capacity for personal faith (Me) has its origin in both your genetics and your cultural upbringing. Modern-day science estimates that 50 percent of who you are is based on your genetics. The DNA passed on to you by your parents and the four hundred thousand years of human generations before them, make up half of the composition of your personality. It's what you've got to work with, and there's nothing you can do about it.

Now it's the other 50 percent that is a bit more interesting because it is totally predicated by the environment we grow up in and the choices we personally make within those surroundings. Since birth most of us have lived with parents, siblings, and relatives who had certain traditions, values, and norms. This group of people you live with are located in a geographical location that has a dominant culture,

"God didn't promise days without pain, laughter without sorrow, or sun without rain, but He did promise strength for the day, comfort for the tears, and light for the way. If God brings you to it, He will bring you through it."

Unknown

religion, and societal framework. All of these pieces of the puzzle play a role in forming your personality, character, and temperament. To exist within a social system, one must conform to the norms and values of that system. The level of faith you have in yourself today was determined by the genetics of your birth and the human interactions that followed ever since.

Don grew up in an Irish family where the gift of storytelling and the personal attention it brought you was a part of daily life. Don's father was a traveling salesman, and whenever he returned home, it was a free-for-all among all the siblings to see who could grab Dad's time and attention. In his early years, Don interacted with the world for the sole purpose of receiving approbation and praise in return. He was always asking himself: "What do people think of me? Do they like me? Do they think I'm funny and a great person to be with?" This yearning for self-affirming feedback became an addiction for Don and eventually approached neurosis. The obsession finally came to a screeching halt when Don began second-guessing the sincerity of the compliments people were showering on him.

Maturity and true friends helped Don move beyond his personal paradox and begin approaching life with a new paradigm. Don realized that his perception of his personal worth and value could no longer be measured by the response of the people around him. He needed to be strong enough, courageous enough, and worthy enough to love himself just for being who he is. He had to have faith in himself and accept the fact that someone might not like him and might not enjoy his colorful storytelling.

There are strong indications that personal faith in our society is in a continuous state of decline. Certainly the increased use of drugs, alcohol, and even obesity is evidence of this downturn. The National Council on Alcoholism and Drug Dependence, Inc. and The Centers for Disease Control and Prevention state:

"Let the first act of every morning be to make the following resolve for the day:
- *I shall not fear anyone on Earth.*
- *I shall fear only God.*
- *I shall not bear ill will toward anyone.*
- *I shall not submit to injustice from anyone.*
- *I shall conquer untruth by truth. And in resisting untruth, I shall put up with all suffering."*

Mahatma Gandhi

- One in every twelve adults abuse alcohol or are alcohol dependent.
- A half million US children between the ages of nine and twelve are addicted to alcohol.
- More than ten million people in the United States abuse prescription medications.
- Over three million in the United States use cocaine.
- Over one million in the United States are in treatment for heroin addiction.
- More than one-third of United States adults are obese.

These statistics are pretty clear: something in the human "Me" equation of energy, focus, and commitment (faith) in daily life is not adding up. We have lost faith in ourselves and our capacity to find meaning and purpose in life. We are repeatedly looking for ways to escape from a world of little faith.

Another tragedy as the result of the downward spiral of personal faith can be seen in the increasing number of suicides throughout the world. Western culture has a strong taboo against any discussion on the subject of death and dying. But the biggest elephant of all elephants in the room that no one ever dares talk about is suicide. Ninety percent of all suicides are caused by a mental illness, the most common of which is depression. According to Dr. Stuart Brown, in his book titled, *Play: How It Shapes the Brain, Opens the Imagination, and Invigorates the Soul*, depression is the opposite of play. No, he didn't say "work" is the opposite of "play"; he said "depression" is the opposite of "play." Brown's research indicates that play helps shape our brain, fosters empathy for others, and is the foundation of creativity and innovation. Everyone could benefit by playing, just for the sake of playing.

So in a culture that defines self-worth by net worth and worthiness by the number of hours you work a week, the present epidemic of depression linked to suicide is an obvious outcome. Depressed people are like those whose ship has lost its rudder. They are no longer connected to the people and the world around them. They have

*"I know in my heart that man is good,
that what is right will always eventually triumph,
and there is purpose and worth to each and every life."*

Ronald Reagan

lost faith in themselves, there is no purpose or meaning to life, and they believe that the world would be a better place without them.

The paradoxical moral of this ugly story is that you are connected to everyone and everything around you. But in order for you to feel that connection, you have to first see it and believe it. Everyone needs faith in life: faith in ourselves, faith in others, and faith in what the future will bring. Researcher, author, and speaker Brene Brown has dedicated her career to exploring the human condition by interviewing thousands of people about their lives and relationships. The results of her work have created the following definition of faith:

Faith is a place of mystery, where we find the courage to believe in what we cannot see and the strength to let go of our fear of uncertainty . . . Get Deliberate; Get Inspired; Get Going!

When the focus of faith shifts to the "We" level, where two or more people unify their faith beliefs, Western society has a tendency to associate the word with some sort of God or religious doctrine. Oftentimes we see images of people gathered in a church or synagogue praying or participating in devout rituals. These groups conduct religious ceremonies like baptisms, communions, and bar mitzvahs as a part of their worship traditions. Faith connects the believer to trusting in a higher power of someone or something that is given complete responsibility for what the future will bring. This belief system provides meaning and purpose in daily life and in the life hereafter.

A simpler form of "We" faith is evident in the institution of marriage. If you are living in the United States and are considering marriage, you truly need faith. According to the Enrichment Journal on divorce rates in America, you might as well flip a coin to see if any married couple will be together five years after the honeymoon. People marry for many reasons, including legal, social, sexual,

"You must not lose faith in humanity.
Humanity is like an ocean;
if a few drops of the ocean are dirty,
the ocean does not become dirty."
Mahatma Gandhi

emotional, financial, spiritual, and religious reasons. Marriage, like the rest of society, is constantly transforming and evolving. Faith in yourself, faith in your partner, and faith in what the two of you will become is more important than ever, to give yourself any chance to weather the storms of time and change.

The final destiny in any faith journey begins with me, it grows to become we, and together it develops into what will be. A person enters the world, meets and commits to a partner, and eventually the two of them unite to create a new life that will start the entire process over again. You must believe in yourself, your energy, focus, and commitment, to take action in life. With personal faith as your foundation, you can reach out to others and together discover your unified creative power and ability to choose a direction and purpose in life together. Finally, your unified dreams, knowledge, and determination will allow you to explore the unknown and to make new discoveries in the future, fulfilling your destiny, and legacy in life.

Faith Journey Dance Steps (From Self to Others):

1. Self-Awareness, Recognition, Acceptance
- *Secrets*
- *Drama & Trauma*
- *Joy & Fun / Pain in the Butt*
- *Heroes & Hooligans*

2. Defining Roadblocks:
- *Fears*
- *Excuses*
- *Control by Others*

3. Strengthening Faith:
- *Commitment / Resolve*
- *Principles / Values*
- *Respect / Trust / Desire for Growth / Confidentiality*

Faith: Duane's Leap of Faith

"Faith is the belief in, a complete trust and confidence in, someone or something that is not immediately provable. Faith is a reservoir of harnessed creative power and energy that provides meaning and purpose to your existence. Without faith in yourself, in others, or in a higher power or greater purpose, you will not fully achieve your destiny and cosmic legacy."

Duane Kuss & Don Calhoun

Dance with the Elephant: Life's Cosmic Equation

Don and I meet once a month with a group of four persons who call themselves a COT group or "Circle of Trust." The purpose of the group is centered around the same four pillars of support described at the beginning of this book: respect, trust, desire for growth, and confidentiality. It was at one of our monthly meetings that I challenged Don to meet with me at five o'clock on a Thursday morning to explore the possibility of writing a book together. We agreed to meet a minimum of four consecutive Thursdays and after that decide if we had the workings of a book and a reason to continue our efforts together.

My purpose in life has always been to explore and discover. I could be called a twenty-first-century Christopher Columbus with the only difference being, instead of sailing the ocean blue, I explore the internet! Every day, via e-newsletters, group emails, RSS feeds, Facebook exchanges, Twitter entries, Google searches, and live webcasts, I surf the internet exploring myriad topics that interest me. As a writer, speaker, consultant, and publisher, I track a wide range of subjects daily. You might think of me as a self-contained media network. It's my Creative Power that inspires me to explore, discover, and apply new ideas, concepts and technologies I learned online.

Don and I have known each other for more than a decade. Don's granite memorial company was one of my customers when I first launched my DigElog online publishing network. More recently, we have become best friends primarily through our monthly COT group meetings. Don has been involved with monument sales all of his professional career. He holds true to his Irish heritage by capturing his clients' attention with delightful stories, always intermixed with his wonderful sense of humor. Don is a storyteller and has always dreamed of combining his stories together into the chapters of a book.

It was the morning of the COT group's monthly meeting in October 2011. I was working in my home office on Hermit Lake and that morning I was

"All truth passes through three stages.
First, it is ridiculed.
Second, it is violently opposed.
Third, it is accepted as being self-evident."

Arthur Schopenhauer

viewing a web video series on information product design, including the topics of course development and book design. One of the guest speakers was from Israel, and he caught my attention when he promised to share his step-by-step process for writing an entire book in a single week. That evening, at the COT meeting, Don once again embellished a story and concluded his entertaining narrative with his favorite cliche, "You know, some day I really should write a book!" But this time, instead of the group placating Don with nodding heads, I shifted forward in my chair and looked Don direct in the eye.

"Don, I have heard you use that phrase a hundred times, if I have heard it once. It's time to make your dream come true. I have discovered a way to help you write your book," I said.

Okay, so what does this long-winded story have to do with the cosmic equation topic of faith? And how is it that I would think I could help Don write a book, when neither of us had any previous training or experience in knowing what it would take?

The answer and evidence can be witnessed in this story by my taking a leap of faith. Even though I had no rational reason or evidence to indicate that Don or I could research, write, design, and publish a book, I had "faith" that our time together would result in something positive. We both had faith that at the very minimum our experience together would bring purpose and meaning to our own lives.

Over the next eighteen months, Don and I not only developed the one hundred topics for four books but also discovered a new way of defining the journey of life itself. Think about it: two slightly above-average family guys, a techie and a monument salesman, living in the land of Lake Wobegon, come together for a few five o'clock breakfasts and in the process discover a simple way of describing

"Be at war with your vices, at peace with your neighbors, and let every new year find a better person."

Benjamin Franklin

humanity's role in the universe. Together we dreamed up three simple equations based on the "Me," "We," and "What Will Be" contribution every human being makes in the world. Three equations that explain the creation of each individual's Cosmic Legacy in the universe.

Don and I had faith that our combined Creative Power and personal experience with Receptive Choice would magically guide us into the unknown future and eventually bring us to a point of discovery worth writing about. Now, whether you agree or disagree with the principles presented in this book, which introduce life's three equations to the world for the first time, most people would have to agree that the chance that any of this would be created by two slightly above-average Lake Wobegon guys is a miracle unto itself. And faith played a critical role in the entire process!

If you are a person of religious or spiritual faith, understanding the kind of faith Don and I had in each other may seem quite trivial. In order for anyone to have a faith and belief in a religion requires a certain amount of trust in the unknown and undefined. There's a piece of every religion that requires faith because there are no tangible answers or proofs of its doctrines and mandates. Don and I had complete faith, trust, and confidence that our journey had a definite purpose in our lives. We also believed that the results of our efforts would at the very least make a difference in our personal lives, even if we failed at writing and publishing our book.

Don's Footnote

The faith that Duane demonstrated in me was a living example of Life's Cosmic Equation in my own life. Without Duane, I believe I would still be dreaming of someday starting this project. My lack of personal faith would have prevented me from ever taking action. In terms of my Life's Cosmic Equation, faith was the essential piece of the equation I was lacking. The other magical realization this

"Act as though it were impossible to fail."

Ralph Waldo Emerson

experience provided me was the fact that I received my faith from someone else. In religious circles they always talk about the church, not as a building, but as a faith community. The faith community is important, because through it, you can both give and receive faith. I will always be grateful that Duane was in the faith-giving mood and I was open to accepting it!

"Because Your Life Is Worth It!"

Digging deeper and growing deeper in faith,
in yourself and others,
has the infinite capacity to change negative social patterns
to positive ones.

Faith: Don's Magical Roller Coaster

*"It is hard to fail; but it is worse
never to have tried to succeed."*

Theodore Roosevelt

Nine months and five days after Katie and I exchanged wedding vows, we welcomed our new son Jonathon into the world. It was a scary, uncertain time, where the two of us wondered how we would measure up to this crazy thing called parenting. With no owner's manual to follow, Katie and I had faith that somehow we could reach beyond how our parents raised us and some way make life even better for our kids.

Neither Katie nor I had ideal family situations growing up. In my family there were essentially two rules to abide by: The first rule, established by my blind mother, was to always let her know where I was and when I would be coming home at night. The second rule was created by my older brother Bob (fourteen years my elder) who stated, "If the goal is to raise a son or daughter to be fully independent, responsible, and free-thinking by the time they turn eighteen, then as parents, you need to give your children as much freedom, responsibility, and ability to experiment in life on their own, as early as possible." Bob's philosophy was that if we demonstrate faith in our kids at an early age and actively support them through the bumps and bruises of making their own choices while growing up, our children will grab the reins of independence much sooner in life and with greater personal success.

Katie and I applied these two principles when raising our son Jonathon and our daughter Michelle. As two young parents we used our Receptive Choice, many times in total conflict with the free advice provided by friends and relatives, and had faith in our instincts in choosing how to raise our children.

Early on in our journey of parenting, Katie and I added two more guideposts to our model, which included high expectations of performance and a commitment to quality time together as family. When it came to high expectations, Kate and I always used positive-active language with our children. It was never a case of "If you go to college." The choice was assumed verbally: "When you go to college."

*"To live is the rarest thing in the world.
Most people exist, that is all."*

Oscar Wilde

We always fed our children with an amazing supply of faith in their individual capacity to learn, grow, and be everything they wanted to be. Jonathon and Michelle were accepted for their personal differences, and they were encouraged to develop their unique Creative Power and interests. As a family we spent quality time together through family meals, specially planned outings, playing games and sports in the backyard, being active members as an entire family at church on Sundays and other gatherings throughout the week, supporting the kids' involvement at school functions and sports events, going on special family trips and planned time together on holidays. As parents, Katie and I made a special effort to be actively involved with our children's curiosities, passions, and dreams. We even allowed our son at twelve years old to run a bobcat and proceed to rip up our yard to create a magical nine-hole pitch and putt golf course!

I am a rather sentimental man and one of my proudest moments as a father came when my son Jonathon, at eighteen years of age, approached me on a Saturday morning asking what I was going to do that day. Jonathon continued, "Dad, let's go golfing and spend some time together. I just love being with you." The two of us had a magical day together. We shared stories about friends, college days, and life in general. At a time when most teenagers rebel against their parents, my son demonstrated friendship, wisdom, and love, well beyond his years.

Well, as grandma used to say, "the proof is in the pudding." Katie and I believed that we would be successful parents if our children were actively pursuing and achieving their dreams. Did our kids take responsibility for their lives and learn to love themselves and others? According to this definition, Katie and I today see ourselves as successful parents. But the truth is, for the most part, our children did most of the work on their own. As parents, we just applied a simple four-part formula and a whole lot of faith.

So what does it take to be a successful parent? What are the guideposts by which

*"Start by doing what is necessary,
then what is possible,
and suddenly you are doing the impossible."*

St. Francis of Assisi

you personally measure success or failure? Is it a college degree, a wife and two kids, a six-figure income, or maybe a five thousand square-foot home in the suburbs? The benchmarks for parental success are all in the mind of the beholder. It's another part of your Receptive Choice and is uniquely constructed by every parent based on their family upbringing, personal experiences, education, and societal norms. It is faith that carries you through the tough times of raising kids, regardless what your parameters of success might be.

Faith is a matter of belief and choice in life. It can be applied to every part of human existence. It is a gift and a ticket to ride the magic roller coaster of your life's journey. Having faith in yourself, in the people you love, and in the world you live in will allow you to discover your true purpose, choose your destiny, and establish your authentic cosmic legacy. Faith will help insulate you from the ever-present emotional demons: guilt, shame, blame, and disconnectedness. It will link you to the positive guideposts of love, trust, and respect in people and will expand your desire for growth in life to higher levels of integrity. You have it within your power to have faith in the present moment and in the future. The choice, as always, is yours.

As parents we were faced with the decision: should we allow our son to explore his faith in his dreams, even if it meant digging our backyard?

Our answer was validated by this magical golf hole that was designed, created, and built by our son Jonathon when he was only twelve years old.

Faith Exercises and Questions

"To have faith is to be sure of the things we hope for, to be certain of the things we cannot see."

Hebrews 11:1

Faith Unleashed: Think back over your life where you have demonstrated faith and commitment to others. It may be helpful for you to think of your best friend, your closest family member, or a spiritual relationship with your creator. Reflect back on the following questions:

Why did you choose to risk and trust in your relationship with this individual?

What benefits in life have you witnessed by demonstrating faith in others?

How did the "give and take" strengthen your connection to each other?

What unique life experiences have you had because you risked the unknown?

Who are three people you have total faith in and would trust even with your life?

What is one thing that you could do today, or this week, to reaffirm your faith and trust in others?

Faith Inhibited: Look back on a time in your life when you felt totally isolated and removed from the world. A time when your faith and commitment to yourself and others was wavering. Examine moments where you made excuses and did not follow through with your responsibility to others. Again, it may be helpful to think of a past friend or family member that you hurt and disappointed, or maybe they caused pain and suffering in your life. Answer the following questions:

Why did you feel helpless and/or hopeless?

What were the key factors and events that led up to your anxiety?

Who were the key actors and what role did they play in the turmoil?

What role did loss of faith and trust have in the scenario?

How did the opinions and perceptions of others influence your actions?

What if you could refill the hourglass of time and do it all over again? What would you change?

Who is responsible when you or someone you trust falls short of your expectations?

What part did shame, guilt, blame, and remorse play in the feelings you have today?

Faith Understood: The purpose of this personal journey back in time was to reacquaint you with the role of faith, trust, and commitment in your life. Having faith or losing faith is a choice we make every day. Your life is lived not in isolation but rather in unity and connection with others. Having a strong faith in yourself, in the people around you, and in the creative destiny of the universe is a key step toward achieving your true Cosmic Legacy. The following questions are meant for your further exploration into the power of faith:

The biggest unknown in life is when the Angel of Death will arrive. To live each day requires a certain level of faith that you'll survive the day and live to see another. How do you feel about the big "D" word (death) and the reality of it as a part of your daily life?

What's the biggest risk you have ever taken in life?
* Got a new job?
* Got married?
* Had children?
* Started a new company?
* Spoke in front of a thousand people?
* Jumped out of an airplane?

How would you finish this sentence: "I passionately have faith in…"?

What dominant values and beliefs did you learn from your parents?

What actions and behaviors did you find empowering within your family?

Do you trust others? When? Where? How? How about yourself?

Do you trust, respect, and have faith in yourself?

When is the last time you stood up for your beliefs, in spite of the objections of others?

How do you react when people disagree with you? Do you get defensive or overreact?

Do you have the ability to look in the mirror and be honest with yourself about your strengths and gifts?

Can you freely identify and admit your weaknesses, shortcomings, and faults?

Does the past determine your future? Do you have the ability to change?

Complete this sentence: "I have faith, hope, and courage that …"?

Seek out one person in the next week who was a mentor in your life. Contact them personally and share with them how grateful you are that they cared to make a difference in your life.

Learn more about Faith at DancewiththeElephant.org

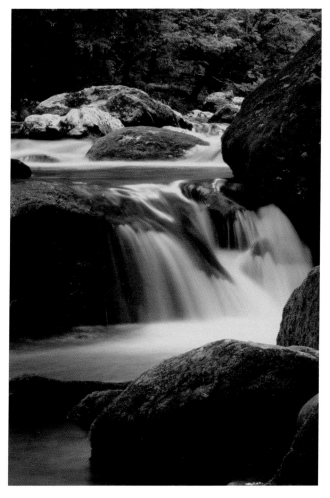

Where Does Your Faith Journey Lead You?

Time

"All the darkness in the world cannot extinguish the light of a single candle."

St. Francis of Assisi

Dance with the Elephant: Life's Cosmic Equation

TIME
THE FOURTH PART OF LIFE'S COSMIC EQUATION

$$\left(\text{Creative Power} + \text{Receptive Choice} + \text{Faith} \right) \times \text{Time} = \text{Your Cosmic Legacy}$$

Time is the fourth and final part of Life's Cosmic Equation. It is the great multiplier that gives action, motion, and movement to the cosmic trinity (Creative Power, Receptive Choice, Faith). Time is the horse that your cosmic trinity rides on in pursuit of your cosmic destiny in the universe. It is the one variable in the equation that you have absolutely no control over. Use it wisely and your greatest dreams can be realized. Take it for granted and lose all direction and purpose in life.

Time is the dimension by which historical events are given order, past through the present and on into the future. It gives the measure of duration that takes place in a single event and the description of the intervals between multiple events. In Western culture, we have a tendency to take time for granted and always look to the future, a future that is rarely reached. We're often surprised when the cradle of life, called death, gets in the way of our goals and dreams. Time has purpose and meaning, as it relates to the past and the action that takes place in the here and now.

As it relates to the human condition, time is what you have between birth and death. The only certainty you can rely on is that the end of life will come, by accident or by body failure. Your time is what it is; you have very little control over it. Accepting death as a part of the package is critical to understanding time's role

"Life can only be understood backwards;
but it must be lived forwards."

Soren Kierkegaard

in Life's Cosmic Equation. If your time is limited, you have a greater motivation to unify your cosmic trinity and develop a greater sense of direction in your life. Life is about taking action and not waiting for it to happen.

In Life's Cosmic Equation, time isn't just about you (the "Me"); it's about you and your interaction with the world around you (the "We"). How well you apply your cosmic trinity in the present moment will directly impact your ability to connect with others who can complement your actions. When the creative power, receptive choice, and faith of two or more people is unified, there exists the capacity to produce exponential results in your lives together and throughout the universe itself.

It doesn't matter whether you live twenty years or a hundred years. Your Cosmic Legacy will be fulfilled. The results of that legacy may vary, but the legacy will exist, nevertheless. Time has the power to provide a sense of urgency and direction in your life. Time is like a compass that always points in the right direction. Time moves on as a constant; we cannot slow it down, nor can we speed it up. Time, like a river, just continues to flow. We cannot determine the length of our life, but we can control our focus, perception, direction, and action.

For the most part, we live in a culture that ignores the existence and reality of death. According to Ernest Becker, we live life either trying to avoid death or finding ways to gain immortality. Unfortunately, up to now, there is no "Get Out of Jail FREE!" card for death and dying. Death is one of the "elephants" in life, from which you could truly benefit, by learning to dance with the elephant. Ponder for a moment the answers to these empowering questions:

* What if you had twenty-one days to live? What nine things would you do if money was no object?

"To live in the moment is to quiet the mind of the past, the uncertainties of the future, and to absorb the essence of the moment like a sponge. Awesome blessings await those who have the capacity to soak up the emotions, feelings and knowledge of a moment."

Don Calhoun & Duane Kuss

* Who would you see, what would you do, and where would you go given the fact you have only twenty-one days left?

* As you look at your list of nine things, is there something you should be doing today? Remember, time is a gift that can be taken away instantly, without warning!

"Space-time" is a term usually used by cosmologists and physicists when they describe the location of objects in the universe. It combines the three spacial dimensions of length, width, and height with the fourth dimension of time. Rather than identifying a location of an object on a three-dimensional grid, the additional dimension of time creates what is known as an "event." The object is given both a where and a when coordinate, describing its place in the universe at a given moment in time. The night sky has 13.7 billion years of history connected to it. The light you see from a given star may have taken billions of years to reach the earth and that moment can be described as a space-time event.

Life's Cosmic Equation is also built on four dimensions, with time as the common thread. Your life is an event in the cosmos, with a given direction, purpose, and outcome to be witnessed. Your story is a space-time story, and you have a unique place in the universe to fill. You bring meaning and significance to the world. Your time is now and now is your time! You, and only you, can create your life event.

"So when I look up at the night sky I know that we are a part of this universe. We are in this universe. But perhaps more important than both of those facts is that the universe is in us. When I reflect on that fact, I feel big because my atoms came from those stars."

Astrophysicist Dr. Neil DeGrasse Tyson

Time: Don's Father Ray Baby

*"Our greatest glory is not in never falling,
but in rising every time we fall."*

Confucius

Dance with the Elephant: Life's Cosmic Equation

It had been months since my mother Edie had passed away. I was still in college but was getting ready to move into my own place for the first time. My father, Ray, still lived at the homeplace but was soon to remarry his new love, Rosemary. Dad and I were in the backyard together that early spring day, enjoying the fresh air and dark green grass. I turned to my father and said, "Dad, I want to thank you for providing me a lovely home to grow up in, for being a great teacher of working hard for what you want in life, and for being a wonderful father." A tear appeared in the corner of dad's eye, and for a rare instant, my father choked up and could not respond. It was at that very moment at the age of twenty-two years old, I first realized the deep love my father had for me.

My father was affectionately known as "Ray Baby." Ray Baby was a larger-than-life character that was true to his father's Irish heritage. He stood for hard work, strong Catholic morals, flamboyant storytelling, infectious roaring laugh, and a bountiful capacity for chugging down his favorite barley pop, always in the company of good friends. Ray Baby could light up the room with his mere presence. His warm, charming, and jovial disposition captured your attention and made you feel better about yourself when you were with him. Dale Carnegie himself could have learned a few things from Ray Baby on how to win friends and influence people.

Ray Baby was one of thirteen children who grew up during the depression in a home where his dad was a hard-working Irish butcher and his mom was a tough old German who didn't take crap from anybody, let alone her children. After doing his part in World War II, Ray Baby returned home and found a job with a local monument company as a salesman. Every Monday, he'd hit the road calling on grieving widows and widowers across Northern Minnesota using newspaper obituaries for his contact information. Every Thursday, he'd return home to finish the week with local sales and paperwork. Ray Baby quickly honed his skills in the monument sales process. He learned how grieving people like to be treated, the

*"Nothing in life is to be feared,
it is only to be understood.
Now is the time to understand more,
so that we may fear less."*

Marie Curie

Dance with the Elephant: Life's Cosmic Equation

comforting words they like to hear and how easily they can be guided into the purchase of a monument for their loved one. He soon became known by his peers and family as the "guy who can sell snowballs to Eskimos."

Ray Baby spent every Thursday night playing cards and partying with the guys. Friday and Saturday were tied up in local sales, so it wasn't until Sunday that any real time was spent with family. The Sunday ritual included the entire family attending church together in the morning, followed by dinner at a local restaurant, providing mom a welcome moment of respite from cooking in the kitchen. Sunday afternoon again shifted back to Ray Baby's World, where he attended a professional sports event or headed out for a round of golf. On occasion, one or more of the children were invited to partake in my father's Sunday afternoon sports outings.

It doesn't take a rocket scientist to predict that us children craved our father's time and attention. We adored his larger-than-life character, and we admired his reputation as the guy everyone looked up to and adored. Early on, I learned that if I joined my father on the road, I could grab some much-needed time and attention with him. Ray Baby would often cart me along with him into some grieving widow's home. Later on, as I grew older, I came to realize that Ray Baby's real motivation for having his son join him was less about spending time together as it was about closing the deal. I was the perfect bait for quickly gaining the widow's trust and hooking another monument sale.

I eventually learned that my silver-tongued father had a gaping hole beneath his charming veneer. The hole was called "sincerity" and "integrity." One of Ray Baby's favorite sayings in working with clients or friends, was "Sweet Baby." I witnessed my father using his "Sweet Baby" charm and magic over and over again. I often witnessed my father talking with people in a completely convincing manner, acting like they were as a long lost friend. Later, Ray Baby would turn to

*"I would rather walk with a friend in
the dark than alone in the light."*

Helen Keller

me and ask, "Son, who was that I was talking to? Do you remember what their name was?"

Do you have someone in your life from whom you long for time and attention?

Do you have someone who always tells you how special and important you are, but you don't really believe them?

Earlier in the chapter on faith, we addressed my early adulthood need for approbation and praise. It's now easy to understand how this desideratum became an integral part of my life. Ray Baby told me repeatedly that "I was the greatest guy God ever let put on a pair of shoes." During each of the sales calls I did with my father, he would praise and affirm me with the greatest accolades. Yet the truth was, at the end of the day, I never believed a single thing my father said about me.

The gift witnessed in a person leaving their family home and journeying out on their own is the fact that it becomes a springboard to applying their Receptive Choice. The experience of growing up and having to make choices can either be an affirmation to follow the same family path or a lightning bolt to discover a new direction. I initially rebelled against my father's insincerity. I made the choice that life could be more than just hard work and making a living. Life was about making true connections with people through repeated moments of shared deep meaning together. I always made it a priority to spend quality time with integrity with my wife and children.

Time now skips forward to when my father, was eighty years old, living in California. My two brothers and I journeyed from the snow-covered tundra of Minnesota to see our father, very possibly for one last magical time together. It was late at night and everyone was in bed except for my dearest father, and myself, his youngest son.

"Tell me and I forget, teach me and I may remember, involve me and I learn."

Benjamin Franklin

During that night, which soon became morning, time stood still for dad and me. The two of us danced with the elephant as we shared stories of love and joy, pain and suffering, hidden secrets and wishes, proud moments, endless regrets. Father and son became one that night. I looked in the mirror and saw my father; Ray Baby looked in the mirror and saw his youngest son. We became kindred souls and eternal exploration partners in the universe. We affirmed and celebrated in the magical journey that life had given us together.

Like all father/son journeys, this story is far from perfect. The story of any two people will always include the binaries of the universe, the yin and yang, the north and south, the good and bad, the heroic and cowardly, the remembered and forgotten. Your Cosmic Legacy will be the composite of yesterday, today, and tomorrow, but it is only today that you can truly affect. Your actions in the moment, right here and now, are the only ones that are important. Spend your time, from this moment forward, as though it were the last moment you would spend in time.

Time: Duane's Auntie Mary

"Time present and time past
Are both perhaps present in time future,
And time future contained in time past.
If all time is eternally present
All time is unredeemable."

T. S. Eliot

I looked out into the congregation and took a moment to identify some of the faces that had gathered for my Auntie Mary's funeral. From the pulpit I could see friends, relatives, and church members who were all there to pay tribute to the extraordinary life of this wonderful woman. Auntie Mary's only son, Wayne, died in a hunting accident when he was thirteen years old. Since that time, I, Mary's godson, had acted as her surrogate son. I now provided the eulogy at her memorial service.

I first got interested in genealogy by listening to stories told by Selma Ziegenhaugen Moore, my grandmother on my mother's side of the family. Grandma Moore told the romantic story of getting to meet Grandpa CR for the first time at a small-town celebration in southern Minnesota. Selma was with her best girlfriend from school, and CR was with a neighborhood kid. CR was the first to spot the two girls standing next to the Ferris wheel. He turned to his friend and said, "I'll bet you a quarter I can get one of those girls over there to take a ride with me on the Ferris wheel." His friend accepted the bet and, of course, lost. I took notes that day as Grandma Moore described a fairy tale —like story of her and CR riding the Ferris wheel, moving to the big city together, and eventually marrying.

But my true passion for family history and storytelling shifted into high gear in 1981, when I joined my godmother, Auntie Mary, on a trip to Blue Earth, Minnesota, the place where my father's family emigrated from Germany to America. Armed with a tape recorder and a 35mm camera, Mary and I interviewed three relatives in three different locations and checked birth records at the county courthouse, all in a single day. It was early that morning, at the farm home of Alvina Kuss Boeck, that the importance of capturing a given moment in time was demonstrated. During the visit, Alvina divulged the existence of a German-language family Bible, a cherished possession handed down to her by her mother, Bertha Ferch Kuss. Inside the Bible were handwritten notes relating

"Lost time is never found again."

Benjamin Franklin

Dance with the Elephant: Life's Cosmic Equation

to family names and birth dates, town names and places of origin back in Germany, and even dates the family's coming to America. I carried the Bible into Alvina's kitchen where the winter sun was the brightest in the house. There, I carefully laid the book out on the kitchen table and methodically took photos of each of the handwritten pages.

Those few handwritten family Bible pages pointed me in the direction that would become a lifelong journey, one that included the discovery of a German family lineage of significant wealth and great hardship. For twenty-one years, I searched for hard evidence that would support the integrity of the handwritten notes. Could I in any way verify the port of departure, port of entry, ship's name, and dates that would document my ancestors arriving in America. The true test of my research would be to discover a ship's log that would specifically reference a family member by name and age. Ship logs can be a major research project unto themselves. People who came across from Europe speaking different languages often misspelled their names, misrepresented themselves as to their occupation and age, and sometimes purposely changed their true identification based on what they believed would provide them the easiest entry into the United States.

It was on Thursday, February 1, 2001, when I finally unlocked the mystery. Twenty-one years after Mary and I ventured to Blue Earth, I discovered the document I had been looking for all this time. It happened at the Mormon Family Research Library in Salt Lake City, Utah. There,

"*Life is but a day:*
A fragile dewdrop on its perilous way
From a tree's summit."

John Keats

among all the family history information collected from around the world, I found the single roll of microfiche that I had been looking for. In a resource center made up of over a million linear feet of film, I found the one square inch that made the total difference for me.

Microfiche publication # 1186
Name of Vessel: Furst Bismark
Port of Embarkation: Hamburg & Southampton
Date of Arrival: August 8, 1891
Passenger #188: Fried Kuss 25 years of age, Male

Can you imagine what that moment was like? I became ecstatic! I grabbed my cell phone and called both my wife Bette and Auntie Mary to let them know the wonderful news. And if that wasn't enough, later that evening I found the ship's log for my great-grandmother Bertha Ferch as well. The Kuss Family History is now in its sixth edition as a 150-page digital book. A Kuss family genealogy website has been published with periodic updates for the past decade. People from all around the world have visited the site and inquiries come about once a month to me.

So as I finished Auntie Mary's eulogy, having shared some of her family heritage story, I left the pulpit with a smile in my heart and a slight grin on my face. There was an elephant in the room that day that very few people would ever know about. What no one knew was that the original Kuss family German Bible no longer exists. Somewhere in the family history that had taken place since that cold winter day in 1981, the Bible with the handwritten notes disappeared. No one knows what happened to it and no one wants to admit that it ever existed. This is an example of where living and capturing the moment changed the course of history for the Kuss family heritage.

Time Exercises and Questions

"I have not failed.
I've just found 10,000 ways that won't work."

Thomas A. Edison

Time Unleashed: Think back over your life to a time that you were fully engaged in your life's mission and purpose. A time when you felt like you were in perfect rhythm and flow with the world around you. You accomplished tasks and things that you never thought were possible. It may be helpful to think of a time when you were a part of a sports team, music group, church retreat, work team, or special project. Reflect on the following questions:

Why were your thoughts and interactions so effortless?

What was your emotional state during this time?

What were you focused on, and what discoveries did you make?

How were your needs being fed, and how did you feed the needs of others?

Was there a special alignment with your Creative Power, Receptive Choice, and Faith?

Who were the people around you, and what connected role did each of them play?

What if you could create experiences like this on a daily basis? What kind of difference would this make in your life and your legacy?

Learn more about Time at <u>DancewiththeElephant.org</u>

Time Inhibited: Remember a time where you were paralyzed with inaction. The trauma in your life was so overwhelming that just to wake up in the morning was an effort. You could have stayed in bed all day wallowing in your sorrows. It may be helpful to think of a time when you felt maligned, mistreated, or unduly judged. Maybe you experienced a great loss: a death, a divorce, or a job change. Please answer the following questions:

Why was this event so different from the normal struggles of daily life?

What were the emotions you felt?

Who did you turn to for support?

What was your internal dialogue?

How did you eventually move on from this significant emotional event or did you?

When dealing with a traumatic life event, how long should it take before getting on with life?

With this life experience now in your past, do you look at life differently today?

Time Understood: The purpose of reflecting back on your times of empowerment and weakness is for you to develop a better understanding of how important it is to purposefully act in the moment. Your time is a gift, and you have a responsibility to use your unique talents to make the world a better place for future generations. The following questions are designed to reconnect you with your mission and destiny in life.

Why did you wake up this morning, and who are you meant to touch today with a kind word of support?

What moments of your childhood were the most powerful in terms of dramatically positive experiences?

What did your most traumatic and painful events of the past teach you?

How can you make a difference in the world today? In a small way? In a big way?

Who are the people in your life who help and encourage you to be your best?

Fear, under control, can be a good thing. How can you leverage your fears today to help motivate you to taking action?

What does it mean for you to live in the moment?

Do you love yourself? Do you love others? How can you be better at sharing your love today?

Are you free to be the child within you? Can you break free from your addictions and harmful habits to just be the magical and extraordinary you!

What could you do today to improve the life of someone you love and in turn bring more meaning into your life?

How will you feed your mind, body, and spirit today so that tomorrow might even be better?

How Are You Committed to This Moment?

Your Cosmic Legacy

"The years teach much the days never know."

Ralph Waldo Emerson

YOUR COSMIC LEGACY

$$\left(\text{Creative Power} + \text{Receptive Choice} + \text{Faith} \right) \times \text{Time} = \text{Your Cosmic Legacy}$$

Your Cosmic Legacy, in its simplest form, is your ability to combine your Creative Power, Receptive Choice, and Faith together, in the amount of time you're given in life, to plant your apple seed and see it grow into the tree it was meant to be and to bear great fruit. But of equal importance is the fact that in order for your legacy to live on beyond your death, someone else has to carry your story forward. Your Cosmic Legacy is more about the relationships and the people you touched in life than it is about the accomplishments or achievements you made. It's less about the "me" of life and more about the "we" of life.

To truly understand Life's Cosmic Equation (WE), we must first revisit the primary equation that precedes it, or Life's Quantum Equation (ME). In the Quantum Equation you add imagination, intuition, and hope together and then multiply the three by action. The quantum result is equal to your life's destiny. With the Cosmic Equation, we are combining the imagination, intuition, hope, and action of two or more people into a unified effort that results in a cosmic legacy. We need our connection to others to help us grow, and we grow most through the experience of helping others grow.

The key to fully manifesting the Cosmic Legacy concept of "we" is to remember that life is not all about you. The greatest impact of your legacy will come from the

*"People are just as happy as they
make up their minds to be."*

Abraham Lincoln

interactions with the people you touched and influenced during your life. It does not matter if you are the president of the United States or a homeless person living under a bridge; the people you touch during your journey in life, your legacy, has equal value and merit. Your story is a part of a constantly evolving story of the universe. In the space-time continuum of the universe, there is no such thing as good and bad, virtue and wickedness, right and wrong, or purposeful and aimless. The universe has a creative destiny that will include your contribution, regardless of the cosmic legacy you choose to leave behind. Each of us has an apple seed to plant. What will be your light bulb? How will your energy shine? What electric connections will you bring to the world around you? And through the connections you make with people throughout your life, how will your light shine even brighter? And finally, upon your death, will your cosmic legacy give rise to even greater connections and energy, leaving a brighter future for the universe?

You and everyone else in this world exists in unity with someone else. There is a connection of energy between all things that is a reality, a constant, an omnipresent link between past, present, and future. We are all connected, not just as fellow human beings, but to the 13.7 billion years of cosmic interaction. Since the beginning of time, what has been created is an infinite, boundless web of connections that tie all things in the universe together. We cannot escape the fact that we are all connected in a cosmic and heavenly way. The question here is not one of creation but one of identification. No one has to create connections to one another; all you have to do is identify the reality that the connections already exist. Together this energy fuses into creative power that inspires new discoveries and gives meaning to life.

We're dancing with another life paradox here: you, as an individual, can successfully apply your imagination, intuition, hope, and actions to achieve your destiny in life, but in the end, following your death, your cosmic legacy will be determined by everyone but you. Your legacy story will be created by the

*"Live simply, love generously, care deeply,
speak kindly. Leave the rest to God."*

Ronald Reagan

people who knew you and connected with your destiny. The legacy that you leave behind will represent the choices, actions, and relationships you cultivated along the journey of life.

Like a single grain of sand that washes up from the ocean floor onto a sandy beach, it may seem as though its destiny is just lost in the multitude. But if you look at the unique journey the grain of sand experienced as it traveled from the bottom of the deep, dark ocean floor and its rise above to become a part of the bright, sunlit, sandy beach, a very different observation can be made. This journey included many collisions with barnacles, sea shells, coral and rock ledges. At one point, the grain of sand was swallowed by a fish and carried for miles in a totally new direction. Each interaction along the way helped to form the size and shape of the sand pebble. In the end, this single grain of sand fulfilled its cosmic legacy to become a part of the complex diversity of pebbles, shells, stones, and other grains of sand that make up the whole of a warm, sandy beach.

We started this book by stating the challenge that only one in ten persons would be brave enough to navigate through the concepts of this book. Congratulations on being one of the chosen few! Now the question is this: what difference can the ideas and principles presented here make in your life and in the lives of the people who are closest to you? What plan of action might you take to help your apple tree grow and bear great fruit? Who are the people you can help to plant their apple seed in fertile ground and nurture them to a life of greater joy and abundance?

In the final analysis, the success or failure of your life's journey is purely a state of mind. On the day you die, the difference between leaving a meaningful legacy or dying like roadkill will exist in your mind only. The pursuit of your destiny will lead to the creation of your legacy based on the priorities you established and the choices you made. Like the pebble of sand that exists as a part of a sandy beach, your life is no less and no more than anything else in the universe. Your destiny is,

*"You can discover more about a person in an hour of play
than in a year of conversation."*

Plato

in your own unique way, to change the universe. Your life, up to now, has done just that: you have changed the universe. You have a purpose to be true to your apple seed. You have a responsibility to contribute to others, that they might grow their own abundant apple tree.

This book has been about asking yourself the right questions. The answers to these questions will provide you a road map to the future. It's time to take control of your destiny and to approach every day with an attitude of gratitude. Every day you can choose to be true to yourself and in concert with those you love and cherish. You have a inner force or guiding spirit that cares for you and is always with you through good times and bad. The world you live in is connected and there is joy to be discovered in your journey to grow and enhance your connectedness with others.

This chapter, in addition to the list of power questions, includes an exercise you can do the next time there's a clear night sky with the stars brightly shining. Life's Cosmic Equation is about sharing life's journey with others. Who are the people in your life who might be in harmony with the guiding pillars of respect, trust, and mutual growth? Can you create a list of two or three people who would enjoy your company and would appreciate the idea of digging deeper in relationships? Make a call, schedule a luncheon date, take action right now that will allow you to grow new branches on your apple tree of life.

Your Cosmic Legacy
Exercises and Questions

*"Never put off for tomorrow,
what you can do today."*

Thomas Jefferson

Your Cosmic Legacy Unleashed: The gift of this exercise requires that you take this assignment very seriously. The more real you can make this activity both mentally and emotionally, the greater meaning and insight it will provide you when you're done. Imagine that you were given the knowledge that you had only twenty-one days left on this earth. The angel of death is coming to take you in twenty days, twenty-three hours, and fifty-nine minutes. Dig deep into your past and present to produce the answers to these questions:

What are you most proud of in your life up to this moment?

Why did you choose the path you followed in your journey?

What positive difference did you make in the lives of the people you loved the most?

Who were your five greatest mentors who helped and directed your destiny?

Who are the twelve people you will invite to your last supper together?

What was your greatest accomplishment in...
> your personal life?
> your family life?
> your career?
> your hobbies?
> your spiritual life?
> fulfilling your destiny?

How will you bring closure to life and meaning to your life?

What purpose and meaning will your life have to the world?

Your Cosmic Legacy Inhibited: Considering the twenty-one days you were given to live at the beginning of this exercise, how much time remains? Have you connected to the emotional reality of your mission here? Throughout this book, we have discussed the trauma of life. Yes, during your final twenty-one days there will be regrets, fears, disappointments, and grief. This part of the assignment might fill you with anxiety. Don't fight it, just push through it, and do your very best to honestly answer the following questions:

Why will your impending death be totally the wrong time and place for you in life?

Why is this not a good day to die?

What three most important dreams or goals in life will you now not be able to achieve?

What would you have done differently now that you know the end is twenty-one days near?

Whom have you wronged in the past and never reconciled with?

Who wronged you in your life and you never forgave them?

How will your death create confusion, anxiety, or distress for those you love?

What would you have done differently if you had the chance to do it all over again?

Your Cosmic Legacy Understood: STOP! Have you successfully filled out your answers to the Cosmic Legacy Unleashed and Inhibited questions on the previous page? If you haven't, do that first before continuing. It is very important to connect with the answers to those questions before you continue. Okay, with the answers in hand, you are ready to complete the twenty-one day exercise. From the answers you have given, you now have the opportunity to do any nine things of your choosing during your final twenty-one days. You can do anything you want, money is no concern, and your only limiting factor is time itself. You must complete all nine events in the time you have left since you began this assignment. If you take a trip to a foreign land, make sure you allocate and subtract the amount of time it will take to get to the place, experience it, and return from it. Remember, you have only the remaining time to put all of your things in order for your impending death. The more real you make the challenge of fitting the pieces together here, the more effective it will be in providing you personal insight and wisdom later on.

1. I choose to…

2. I look forward to…

3. I want to…

4. I will definitely…

5. I absolutely have to…

6. I owe it to…

7. I feel obligated to…

8. I have no choice but to…

9. I am privileged and grateful to...

Learn more about Your Cosmic Legacy at DancewiththeElephant.org

"Why be good? When you can be great!"

Don Calhoun has thirty years of firsthand, real-world experience with understanding the highs, lows, triumphs, and tragedies of life. Calhoun is an owner and president of Murphy Granite Carving, Inc., which produces cemetery memorials throughout the upper Midwest of the United States. Calhoun has been a memorial counselor for numerous families at the time of their heightened emotional grief. He has been a highly sought after speaker in the memorial, monument, and funeral industries throughout the United States and Canada. His many speaking engagements, most recently centered around his forthcoming book with Duane, *Dance with the Elephant,* have received great accolades from audiences all across the country. Calhoun's unique work in the memorial industry, combined with his personal life experience of growing up with a legally blind mother who battled brain cancer until her death, has made Don a professional life storyteller. Don's insights will help you peel back the layers of life and discover your true purpose and destiny. You will learn how to deal with the emotional aspects of life in new empowering ways.

Dare to Dream; Explore Your Passions; Find Your Purpose

Duane Kuss, is a writer, publisher, and lifelong trainer who has over sixteen different professional career experiences over the past four decades. Kuss has been a professional speaker, trainer, and consultant across multiple disciplines. His past clients include Apple Computers, Thrifty White Pharmacy, Potlatch Corporation, the Minnesota Newspaper Association, and the Journal Communications Publishing group. Duane's work with Dr. John Geier and his world famous DISC personality profiling instrument afforded him international exposure and the chance to work with authors like Harvey McKay, Michael Dowd, Connie Barlow, and other key influences. The son of an auto mechanic and a bookkeeper housewife, Kuss decided early in his life that he would become a twentieth century renaissance man, "A man for all seasons." Duane's intellectual and scientific perspective will provide you with analytic insights that will help you to discover your cosmic destiny! You will discover a new passion for learning about your human and heavenly potential.

Your Cosmic Legacy Gift

*"To everything there is a season,
and a time to every purpose under heaven."*

Ecclesiastes 3:1

Your Life's Cosmic Legacy Gift

Take the list of nine events you created and commit to doing them over the next nine days, nine weeks, nine months, or nine years. Make plans immediately to do whatever it takes to accomplish all of these nine most important facets to your future destiny in life. For this is what will create your Life's Cosmic Legacy in the universe.

If Not Now...

When?

The Denial of Death by Ernest Becker

The pinnacle of a life's work and winner of the Pulitzer Prize in 1974, *The Denial of Death* is Ernest Becker's dazzling and profound answer to the "why" of human existence. In courageous opposition to the prevailing Freudian school of thought, Becker tackles the problem of man's defiance to recognize his own death. Becker sheds a fresh and new perspective on the nature of people. His work proclaims a new path to life and living, that stills has a profound echo effect today.

The Gifts of Imperfection: Let Go of Who You Think You're Supposed to Be and Embrace Who You Are by Brené Brown

In *The Gifts of Imperfection,* Brené Brown, a preeminent professional on shame, blame, guilt, authenticity, and belonging, shares ten pillars on the power of Wholehearted living—a way of engaging with the world from a place of worthiness.

The Dream of the Earth by Thomas Berry

This milestone work has established itself as a primary cornerstone in the ecological canon. In it, distinguished cultural historian Thomas Berry implements a new intellectual-ethical framework for the human community by positing planetary well-being as the measure of all human activity. Drawing on the wisdom of Western philosophy, Native America traditions, and Asian thought, as well as contemporary physics and evolutionary biology, Berry offers a new viewpoint that re-frames our understanding of science, technology, politics, religion, ecology, and education. He shows us why it is important for us to respond to the Earth's need for planetary renewal and what we must do to break free of the "technological trance" that drives a misguided dream of progress. Only then, Berry believes, can we champion cooperatively enhancing human-Earth relationships that can rebuild our distressed global bio-system.

The Universe Story: From the Primordial Flaring Forth to the Ecozoic Era; A Celebration of the Unfolding of the Cosmos by Brian Swimme

From the big bang to the present and into the next millennium, *The Universe Story* consolidates science and the humanities in a powerful examination of the unfolding of the universe, humanity's developing place in the cosmos, and the limitless opportunities for our future legacy.

A Brief History of Everything by Ken Wilber

A Brief History of Everything is a welcoming and feasible explanation of our place in a universe of sex, soul, and spirit, written by an author of whom *New York Times* reporter Tony Schwartz says: "No one has described the path to wisdom better than Ken Wilber."

Wilber investigates the course of evolution as the advancing demonstration of Spirit, from matter to life to mind, including the higher stages of spiritual development where Spirit becomes conscious of itself. In each of these domains, there are persistent themes, and by examining them closely, we can understand and learn about the place in the world—and the journey we must take if "global transformation" is to become a truth.

Wilber offers a series of astonishing and unique perspectives on many subjects of relevant interest and controversy, including the gender wars, modern liberation movements, multi-culturalism, ecology, environmental ethics, and the conflict between this-worldly and otherworldly approaches to spirituality. The result is a fascinating journey through the Cosmos.

Thank God for Evolution: How the Marriage of Science and Religion Will Transform Your Life and Our World by Michael Dowd

Few issues have manifested increased disagreement in our world than the debate between creationism and evolution, between religion and science. Reverend Michael Dowd has come forth as a healer, finding faith strengthened by the power of reason. With evidence from contemporary astrophysics, geology, biology, anthropology, and evolutionary psychology, *Thank God for Evolution* demonstrates a imperative dissertation for how religion and science can be harmoniously enriching forces in our lives. Lauded by Nobel laureates in the scientific community and religious leaders alike, *Thank God for Evolution* will expand the possibilities for self, for relationships, and for our world.

Griefwalker (DVD) by Stephen Jenkinson

This Canadian documentary is a rhythmic, fascinating, extraordinary, and even light hearted examination of one's relationship to life and death. The film maker follows his great friend, Stephen Jenkinson, a social worker and clinical care worker who has been the friend and witness to hundreds, maybe thousands, of people on their deathbeds, and their families. The film is like being given approval to join along with these two men as they explore how to live fully, by making their awareness of the end of their lives ever-present instead of overlooked or neglected.

The 5 Love Languages by Gary Chapman

Marriage should have the foundation built on love, right? But does it seem as though both of you are speaking two different languages? *New York Times* bestselling author Dr. Gary Chapman teaches couples in identifying, understanding, and speaking their spouse's primary love language—quality time, words of affirmation, gifts, acts of service, or physical touch.

By learning the five love languages, you and your spouse will discover your unique love languages and learn reasonable and logical methods in really loving each other. Chapters are organized by love language for easy guidance, and each one ends with specific, easy steps to practice a individual language to your spouse and guide your marriage to a deeper and more rewarding relationship. A newly created love languages assessment will help you understand and enhance your marriage.

How to Stop Worrying and Start Living by Dale Carnegie

Learn how to break the worry habit—Now and forever! With Dale Carnegie's timeless advice in hand, more than six million people have learned how to reduce unproductive fear and worry from their lives and to accept a worry-free future. In this master work, *How to Stop Worrying and Start Living*, Carnegie offers a set of practical steps that you can use in your everyday life. It is a book full of lessons that will endure a lifetime and make your life happier!

Awaken the Giant Within: How to Take Immediate Control of Your Mental, Emotional, Physical and Financial Destiny! by Anthony Robbins

Wake Up and Take Control of Your Life! Anthony Robbins, the nation's leader in the science of peak performance, shows you his most effective strategies and techniques for mastering your emotions, your body, your relationships, your finances, and your life. Robbins is a famous and accredited expert in the psychology of change, he provides a clearly laid out program teaching the basic and foundational lessons of self-mastery that will help you to discover your true purpose, take control of your life, and harness the influences that determine your destiny.

Gratefulness, the Heart of Prayer: An Approach to Life in Fullness by Brother David Steindl-Rast

A member of the Calmaldolese Order of monks, and well-known for his far-reaching interests in theology and science, Steindl-Rast does an amazing job of uncovering the relationship between prayer and the sense of gratefulness that comes with love, which is at the very center of what it means to be human.

Action: the fact or process of doing something, typically to achieve a desired outcome. Think of action as applied Energy to a task in a moment of time. Action implies movement in physical, mental or spiritual nature. Action is the great multiplier of your Creative Power, Receptive Choice, and Faith.

Blame: the act of making negative statements, censuring, holding an individual or group responsible, either morally or socially for their actions. Blame is often based on the perceptions and values of the individual or group whether they in fact right or wrong, true or false. The opposite of blame is praise.

Control: to exercise authoritative or dominating influence over one's beliefs or actions. Control in this context can deal with those things having dominating influence over you or it can be with your authoritative influence over others.

Commitment: the state or quality of being dedicated to a cause, activity, or belief. To have commitment is to have Faith which is needed to complete a task, cause, or belief. That commitment can be within yourself, or even a belief outside of yourself. Commitment is also known as a pledge or an undertaking that you fully intend to complete.

Creative Power: is the unique energy source within you. When identified, understood, utilized and acted upon, it will provide you infinite capacity to fully realize your dreams and reach your final destiny.

Cosmic Legacy: is something physical, mental, or spiritual that is passed on by and through you to your family or friends or the world that is immeasurable extended in time and space. Your legacy can include your positive or negative interactions and influences, known or unknown, with others.

Death: is the permanent cessation of all biological/physical functions that sustain a living person / organism.

Destiny: or fate is a predetermined course of events, whether in general or of an individual. Destiny is based on the belief there is a fixed natural order to your Cosmic Legacy. They are your dreams put into action with conviction that manifests and unleashes Creative Power. Your destiny must be owned by your mind, body, and spirit. Destiny is a core goal that you must make a reality.

Dream: personal images, ideas, emotions, and sensations of your mind, body, or spirit, that you wish would manifest themselves into a reality. Your dreams change and evolve overtime. Dreams are the building blocks to finding your Energy and ultimately your Creative Power.

Drama: a positive and rewarding experience that has been a very strong influence on making you who you are. Drama really shapes and defines your values, faith and beliefs.

Echo Effect: is defined as a change in perception of a dramatic or traumatic event overtime. For example: A class in college that was extremely difficult, emotionally and physically taxing at the time, in hindsight, may turn out to be the best learning experience you ever had and the most rewarding.

Energy: (Passion) is an indirectly observed quality that provides you physical, mental, or spiritual means to achieve your destiny. Energy is what motivates you while you are performing a task, or those things that feed your soul for future resource. Think of energy in terms of a battery. What feeds your current energy levels and what replenishes them for your long term reserves?

Excuses: to grant or obtain an exemption for a group of people or yourself, sharing a common characteristic from a potential liability or harm. Excuses may be real or just perceived. Excuses most commonly undermine your Faith in order to complete a task.

Faith: the belief in, a complete trust and confidence in, someone or something that is not immediately provable. Faith is a reservoir of harnessed creative power and energy that provides meaning and purpose to your existence. Without faith in yourself, in others, or in a higher power or greater purpose, you will not fully achieve your destiny and cosmic legacy.

Fear: distressing emotion aroused by impending danger, evil, pain, etc., whether the threat is real or imagined; the feeling or condition of being afraid.

Focus: (cognitive process) is selectively concentrating on one or limited aspects of the knowledge, skills, and tasks needed while ignoring other things.

Gratitude: the quality and active perception of being thankful. Having a willingness and freedom to express, demonstrate and show appreciation for others.

Guilt: is an emotion that occurs within an individual when they believe they have violated their own moral standard. Guilt, like the concept of sin, is going against one's self-conscious beliefs, values and principles.

Heroes and Hooligans: Heroes are those individuals you look up to for positive inspiration. Hooligans are the individuals you observe for the negative behaviors they exhibit, that you do not wish to follow.

Receptive Choice: is the active awareness that you are given the ability to choose and filter how you perceive the world around you. Receptive Choice empowers you to discover the magical path in life, in perfect harmony with your Creative Power. It will set you free from the shackles of judgment by others and it will lead you to beautiful horizons on your unique and personal legacy.

Time: the dimension by which historical events are given order through the past, present and on into the future. It's the measurable duration that takes place in a single event and the description of the intervals between multiple events. Time is the one variable you have no control over, other than your ability to focus, or live in the moment. Time used wisely is your greatest asset that can help you achieve your dreams.

Trauma: is defined as a negative or painful experience that had a very strong influence on making you who you are. Trauma really shapes and defines your beliefs, values and faith.

Secret: knowledge of an event, thought, or belief that is concealed, hidden, or not revealed to others. A secret can be about yourself, family, church, community, country, or the world. It can be real or perceived. A secret can be minor or major, depending on the risk level associated with its revelation.